The Everyday Chef

LIGHT
AND EASY

Published by Celebrity Press
An imprint of Hambleton-Hill Publishing, Inc.
Nashville, Tennessee 37218

Printed and bound in the United States of America

ISBN 1-58029-010-8

10 9 8 7 6 5 4 3 2 1

Graphic Design/Art Direction
John Laughlin

Contents

Conversion Table

Metric Conversions

1/8 teaspoon = .05 ml
1/4 teaspoon = 1 ml
1/2 teaspoon = 2 ml
1 teaspoon = 5 ml
1 tablespoon = 3 teaspoons = 15 ml
1/8 cup = 1 fluid ounce = 30 ml
1/4 cup = 2 fluid ounces = 60 ml
1/3 cup = 3 fluid ounces = 90 ml
1/2 cup = 4 fluid ounces = 120 ml
2/3 cup = 5 fluid ounces = 150 ml

3/4 cup = 6 fluid ounces = 180 ml
1 cup = 8 fluid ounces = 240 ml
2 cups = 1 pint = 480 ml
2 pints = 1 liter
1 quart = 1 liter
1/2 inch = 1.25 centimeters
1 inch = 2.5 centimeters
1 ounce = 30 grams
1 pound = 0.5 kilogram

Oven Temperatures

Fahrenheit	Celsius
250°F	120°C
275°F	140°C
300°F	150°C
325°F	160°C
350°F	180°C
375°F	190°C
400°F	200°C
425°F	220°C
450°F	230°C

Baking Dish Sizes

American	Metric
8-inch round baking dish	20-centimeter dish
9-inch round baking dish	23-centimeter dish
11 x 7 x 2-inch baking dish	28 x 18 x 4-centimeter dish
12 x 8 x 2-inch baking dish	30 x 19 x 5-centimeter dish
9 x 5 x 3-inch baking dish	23 x 13 x 6-centimeter dish
1 1/2-quart casserole	1.5-liter casserole
2-quart casserole	2-liter casserole

Dips & Snacks

Baste:

To brush (or spoon) cooking liquids over food
to prevent it from drying out.

Beat:

To mix ingredients until smooth by using a quick
stirring motion or an electric mixer.

Vegetable Dip

1 c carrots, minced
1 c broccoli florets, minced
1 c cauliflower florets, minced
1/2 c onion, minced
2 pkg (8 oz ea) soft cream cheese
1 tsp dill weed
1/2 tsp ground cumin
1/4 tsp chili powder
5-10 drops hot pepper sauce

Combine all ingredients in food processor. Process until smooth. Refrigerate dip for 1 hour or overnight in covered bowl. Serve with fresh vegetables and crackers.

Super Spinach Dip

2 c nonfat yogurt
1 pkg. frozen chopped spinach, thawed and drained
1/3 c onion, chopped fine
2 tbsp reduced-calorie mayonnaise
1 pkg instant vegetable soup mix

Combine all ingredients in a medium bowl. Serve immediately or cover and chill for up to 3 hours. Serve with chopped vegetables.

Buttermilk Herb Dip

8 oz light sour cream
1/4 c buttermilk
1/2 tsp dill weed
1/4 tsp salt
2 tbsp parsley, chopped
1/4 tsp garlic, minced
1/4 tsp black pepper

Combine all ingredients in mixing bowl. Cover and refrigerate for about 2 hours. Serve with fresh vegetable sticks and crackers.

Cottage Cheese Dip

1 c dry curd cottage cheese
1/2 c buttermilk
1/4 tsp lemon juice
1 pkg dry onion soup mix

Process all ingredients in blender until smooth. Refrigerate for 2 hours or overnight. Serve with fresh vegetables and crackers.

Stuffed Mushrooms

1 lb medium mushrooms, washed, stems removed and chopped
2 tbsp olive oil, divided
1/2 c red bell pepper, chopped fine
1/4 c onion, chopped fine
1/4 c creamy mustard
1/4 tsp garlic powder
1/4 tsp dried oregano, crushed
1 tbsp Parmesan cheese, grated

Put mushroom caps right side up on a foil-lined broiler pan. Brush tops of caps with 1 tablespoon olive oil.

Broil 5 to 10 minutes or until tender. Drain excess oil and set aside.

Heat 1 tablespoon olive oil in medium skillet over high heat. Stir in chopped mushroom stems, bell pepper, and onion and sauté until almost dry.

Add mustard and seasonings. Spoon 1 teaspoon vegetable mixture into each mushroom cap. Sprinkle Parmesan cheese evenly over caps. Broil for 5 minutes or until lightly browned.

Tortilla Pinwheels

1 pkg (8 oz) cream cheese, softened
1 c sour cream
1 c Monterey Jack cheese, shredded
1/2 c pimento-stuffed green olives, chopped
1/2 tsp seasoned salt
1/4 tsp garlic powder
1/4 c red onion, chopped
1 can (15 oz) black beans, drained
five 10-inch flour tortillas

Beat cream cheese and sour cream in bowl until well blended. Stir in Monterey Jack, olives, salt, garlic powder, and onion. Cover and refrigerate for two hours. Process beans in food processor or blender until smooth. Spread each tortilla with thin layer of beans. Spread thin layer of cream cheese mixture over beans. Roll up tortillas tightly. Wrap in plastic wrap and refrigerate until chilled. Cut tortillas into small slices.

Cheese and Rice Squares

2 c cooked rice
1 c low-fat cheddar cheese, shredded
1/2 c onion, minced
3 tbsp all-purpose flour
1/2 tsp salt
1/2 tsp black pepper
3 egg whites
1/8 tsp cream of tartar

Combine rice, cheese, onion, flour, salt, and pepper in mixing bowl. Beat egg whites with cream of tartar in small bowl until stiff. Fold beaten egg whites into rice mixture. Spoon 2 to 3 tablespoons batter per square into a non stick skillet or one that has been sprayed with cooking spray. Cook over medium heat until golden brown on both sides. Serve warm with sour cream.

Spicy Rice Balls

2 c cooked rice
1 pkg (10 oz) frozen spinach, thawed, drained, and squeezed dry
2/3 c dry Italian bread crumbs, divided
1/2 c Parmesan cheese, grated
1/3 c onion, minced
3 egg whites, beaten
1/4 c skim milk
1 tbsp Dijon mustard

Preheat oven to 375° F. Toss spinach, rice, 1/3 cup bread crumbs, cheese, onion, egg whites, milk, and mustard in a large bowl. Shape mixture into 1-inch balls. Roll each ball in remaining bread crumbs. Place on baking sheet coated with cooking spray. Bake for 10 to 15 minutes until browned.

Crunchy Ranch Chicken Fingers

1 c cornflake crumbs
1 tbsp fresh parsley
1/3 c Ranch dressing
1 tsp water
1 lb. boneless, skinless chicken breasts, cut into thin strips

Preheat oven to 425° F. Combine cornflake crumbs and parsley in small bowl. Combine ranch dressing and water in another small bowl.

Dip chicken in dressing mixture and then in cornflake mixture. Lightly spray a baking pan with cooking spray.

Bake 8 minutes or until chicken is tender.

Light Herbed Rice Cake

1 c medium-grain rice
1 tsp salt
2 c water
4 tbsp butter, melted
1 c cheddar cheese, grated
2 tbsp onion, chopped fine
2 tsp dried dill
1 egg, lightly beaten
1/2 c milk
1/4 tsp hot pepper sauce
1/8 tsp black pepper

Preheat oven to 350° F. In a medium saucepan, combine rice, salt, and water. Bring to a boil over high heat. Cover tightly, reduce heat to lowest setting, and cook for 15 to 18 minutes or until rice is tender but still slightly firm. Remove from heat and fluff rice with fork.

In a large mixing bowl, combine butter, cheese, onion, dill, egg, milk, hot pepper sauce, and black pepper, blending well. Add rice and toss to combine.

Press mixture evenly into a lightly buttered 8- or 9-inch square baking dish. Bake in center of oven for 35 to 45 minutes, until rice begins to brown lightly around edges and becomes crusty. Remove from oven and let cool for 20 minutes before cutting. Run a small knife around edges of dish and cut rice into 2-inch squares.

Light Fiesta Shrimp Dip

10 oz frozen cooked shrimp
1/3 c green onions, chopped fine
1 pkg light cream cheese, softened
2/3 c picante sauce
2 tsp horseradish
1/4 c light mayonnaise
3/4 tsp ground cumin

Finely chop shrimp, reserving a few whole shrimp for garnish. Combine cream cheese and mayonnaise; mix well. Reserve. Stir all remaining ingredients except 1 tablespoon green onions into cream cheese mixture; mix well. Spoon into serving bowl. Chill for at least 2 hours or up to 24 hours. Stir; garnish with reserved shrimp and green onions. Serve with assorted vegetable sticks.

Luscious Orange Bars

1 tsp unflavored gelatin
1/4 c frozen orange juice concentrate, softened
2 tbsp sugar
1/2 tsp vanilla
1/2 c nonfat dry milk powder
1/2 c cold water
1 tbsp lemon juice
24 graham crackers

Soften gelatin in orange juice in top section of a double boiler. Stir until gelatin is completely dissolved.

Remove from heat and stir in sugar and vanilla.

Chill a small mixing bowl and beaters. Using cold beaters, beat dry milk and water until soft peaks form.

Add lemon juice and beat until stiff. Fold in orange juice mixture. Spread on 12 graham crackers. Top with remaining crackers.

Wrap individually and freeze until firm, about 2 hours.

8

Lime Chicken Strips

3 lb skinless and boneless chicken breasts,
   cut into 1/2 x1 1/2-inch strips
6 oz frozen limeade concentrate, softened
2 tbsp lime zest, minced
6 garlic cloves, minced

Combine all ingredients in a large mixing bowl and refrigerate. Marinate overnight.

Preheat oven to 350° F. Pour marinade into a bowl and set aside. Place chicken in a shallow baking dish and bake for 45 minutes. Pour marinade over chicken and bake for another 45 minutes, tossing every 10 minutes to coat thoroughly. Cook until golden brown. Serve hot.

Avocado Delight

2 avocados
Romaine lettuce leaves
1 tsp salt
1/2 tsp white pepper
1/2 tsp dried oregano
1 clove garlic, minced
2/3 c olive oil
1 tbsp red wine
1 tbsp vinegar

Cut avocados in half and discard pits. Scoop out avocado meat with an ice cream scoop; shape meat into little balls. Place balls on two plates lined with lettuce leaves. In a small bowl, whisk together remaining ingredients; pour over avocados and serve.

Baked Oysters

1/4 lb butter
1 onion, chopped fine
2 c celery
1 pt oysters, chopped
1 c oyster juice *or* water
2 c bread, toasted and crumbled
4 eggs, hard-boiled and grated
parsley
salt and pepper to taste
cracker crumbs

Melt butter; add onion and celery and cook until tender. Add oysters and half of liquid; cook about 5 minutes or until oysters curl. Remove from heat; mix in bread crumbs, grated eggs, and parsley. Add salt and pepper; dampen with remaining liquid. Put into oyster shells or greased casserole; sprinkle with cracker crumbs and dot with butter. Bake at 350° F for about 20 minutes.

Veggie Pizza

2 pkg refrigerated crescent roll dough
2 pkg (8 oz ea) regular or light cream cheese
3/4 c mayonnaise
1 pkg dry Ranch dressing mix
5 c vegetables, chopped
1 c cheddar cheese, shredded (optional)

Press crescent roll dough into a large, greased jelly roll pan, sealing all perforations in dough.

Bake according to package directions for about 10 minutes.

Combine cream cheese, mayonnaise, and dressing mix; beat until smooth. Spread cream cheese mixture over cooled crust and sprinkle with chopped vegetables.

Top with shredded cheese if desired. Chill for one hour before serving.

Pork and Scallion Wraps

1/2 lb pork tenderloin
6 scallions
1 clove garlic, crushed
1 tbsp soy sauce
1 tbsp honey
1 tbsp oil
1 tbsp Hoisin sauce
1 tsp fresh ginger root, grated

Trim any excess fat from pork, then cut into 20 round slices. Flatten meat slices with a knife or mallet. Trim roots and any wilted leaves from scallions; cut each scallion into 3 or 4 pieces. Place scallion on a meat slice and roll up. In a shallow baking dish, stir together garlic, soy sauce, honey, oil, Hoisin sauce, and ginger root. Place pork rolls seam-side down in soy mixture; turn to coat. Cover and refrigerate until baking time. Bake, uncovered, at 400° F for 10-15 minutes or until meat is no longer pink in center. Baste rolls frequently with sauce during baking. Serve hot or warm.

Shrimp Sauté

1/2 c oil
1 lb medium shrimp in shells (about 30)
1/2 tbsp salt
1/2 tsp pepper, ground coarsely
1/2 tbsp oregano, crushed
1/2 c onion, sliced thin
1/2 tbsp garlic, mashed
1 whole jalapeño pepper, sliced
juice of 1 lemon *or* of 2 limes

Heat oil in large pan or wok. Add washed, unshelled shrimp and stir-fry for 3 minutes. Add seasonings and jalapeño peppers and stir-fry until blended and heated through. Just before serving, add fresh lemon or lime juice.

Pear and Granola Whole Wheat Muffins

3/4 c pear nectar
2 large eggs
2 tbsp vegetable oil
1 tbsp fresh lemon juice
1 tsp grated lemon peel
1 c whole-wheat flour
1 c all-purpose flour
2/3 c brown sugar
1/2 c low-fat granola
1 tbsp baking powder
1/2 tsp ground nutmeg
1/2 tsp salt
1 1/4 c (about 1 medium) pear, unpeeled, chopped fine

Preheat oven to 350° F. Line muffin pan with foil muffin papers.

Whisk first 5 ingredients in large bowl to blend. Stir both flours and sugar in medium bowl until no lumps remain.

Mix in granola, baking powder, nutmeg, and salt. Add pear; toss to coat.

Stir flour mixture into egg mixture until just blended. (Batter will be thick.) Divide among prepared muffin cups, mounding in center.

Bake muffins until golden brown and tester inserted into center comes out clean (about 20 minutes).

Transfer muffins to rack and cool.

Soups & Salads

Blanch:

To immerse briefly in boiling water.

Boil:

To raise the temperature of a liquid until it bubbles.
The boiling temperature of water is 212° F (or 100° C)

11

Potato Salad

6 large potatoes
French dressing
2 tbsp parsley, chopped
1 tbsp radishes, chopped
1 tbsp chives, chopped
salt and pepper to taste

Cook potatoes in their skins until soft. Peel and dice hot potatoes. Combine with French dressing and other seasonings. Chill and serve cold.

Antipasto Salad With Garlic Dressing

1 can (15 1/2 oz) garbanzo beans, drained
6 1/2 oz marinated artichoke hearts
2 c tortellini, cooked
1/2 c red peppers, roasted
1/4 c black olives, pitted, drained, and sliced
2 bunches romaine lettuce, torn into
  bite-sized pieces
Garlic Dressing (recipe follows)
1/2 c low-fat salami, sliced
1/2 c mozzarella cheese
1/4 c Parmesan cheese, freshly grated

Place beans, artichoke hearts, pasta, roasted peppers, and olives in salad bowl; add lettuce. Pour dressing over all and toss well. Arrange salami on salad greens. Sprinkle with cheeses over top.

Garlic Dressing

2 tbsp olive oil
1 tbsp tarragon vinegar
1/4 tsp prepared mustard
1/4 tsp Worcestershire sauce
1 clove garlic, crushed
1 dash pepper

Combine all ingredients in tightly covered jar and shake.

Black Bean and Rice Salad

2 c canned black beans, rinsed and drained
2 c rice, cooked
1 1/2 c fresh cilantro
1/4 c lime juice
3/4 c oil
1/2 c onion, chopped
2 garlic cloves, crushed
salt
fresh ground black pepper

Mix beans, rice, and cilantro together in a bowl. Place lime juice in a small bowl and whisk in oil. Add onion and garlic; toss with rice and bean mixture. Add salt and pepper to taste.

Lima Bean Salad

1 c dried lima beans, soaked
1 large tomato, diced
2 tbsp olive oil
1 tbsp red wine vinegar
1 tsp maple syrup
salt and pepper to taste
1/2 tsp dry mustard
parsley, chopped

Drain and wash lima beans. Cover with fresh water and cook until soft, about 45-60 minutes. Drain. Combine lima beans and tomato in a serving bowl. Whisk together all remaining ingredients except parsley. Toss dressing with beans and tomatoes. Chill. Garnish with parsley before serving.

Reduced-Fat Waldorf Salad

3/4 lb chicken breast (2 boneless,
   skinless halves), roasted and diced
1 Granny Smith apple, cored and diced
   into 1/2-inch pieces
1 rib celery, minced fine
1 ripe mango, peeled and diced
2 tbsp ginger, candied and minced
1/3 c light mayonnaise
1/3 c nonfat sour cream
2 tbsp lime juice
2 tbsp mango chutney
1 tsp prepared mustard
3 tbsp walnuts, chopped coarse
2 tbsp fresh mint, minced

Combine chicken, apple, celery, mango, and
candied ginger. In a medium bowl combine
mayonnaise, sour cream, lime juice, chutney,
and mustard; mix well. Add to salad, mixing
well. Cover and refrigerate. Just before serving,
stir in chopped walnuts and mint.

Red Potato Salad With Bacon

2 lb red potatoes
1/3 lb bacon, diced
1 c yellow onion, thinly sliced
4 scallions, chopped
1/4 c mayonnaise
1/2 tsp dry mustard
1 tbsp white wine vinegar
1/2 c olive oil
salt and pepper to taste
2 eggs, hard-boiled

Wash and drain potatoes. Using a paring knife,
trim a 1/2-inch wide band of peel from
circumference of each potato. Boil trimmed
potatoes gently in lightly salted water until just
tender. Carefully drain, spread on a tray, and
let cool.

Cook bacon until almost crisp. Add onion; cook
until limp. Drain any excess fat. Place cooled
potatoes in a bowl with cooked bacon and
onion; add scallions. In another bowl, blend
together mayonnaise, dry mustard, vinegar, oil,
and salt and pepper. Add to potatoes and toss
together. Fold in hard-boiled eggs. Cover and
refrigerate.

Rice Salad

2 c rice, cooked
2 c corn kernels
2 c green bell pepper, diced
1 1/2 c kidney beans, cooked
1 onion, chopped
6 tbsp distilled white vinegar
3 tbsp vegetable oil
2 tsp soy sauce
2 tsp prepared mustard
1 tsp prepared horseradish

Mix rice, corn, peppers, kidney beans, and
onion in a bowl. In a smaller bowl combine
vinegar, oil, soy sauce, mustard, and
horseradish; pour over other ingredients.
Toss well.

Apple Cheddar Salad

2 red apples, quartered
2 tsp lemon juice
1/4 c mayonnaise
salt and pepper
2 c celery, diced
6 oz mild cheddar cheese, cubed
lettuce

Place apples in small bowl; toss with lemon
juice. Add all remaining ingredients except
lettuce; toss to coat. Serve on lettuce-lined plate.

13

Pasta Vegetable Chowder

1 c elbow macaroni
3 c milk, divided
1 box (10 oz) frozen mixed vegetables,
  thawed and drained
1/2 tsp dried thyme
1/2 tsp paprika
1 1/2 tbsp cornstarch
1 can (6 oz) clams, drained
salt and pepper to taste

Prepare pasta according to package directions.
Rinse cooked pasta under cold water until cool;
drain. Combine pasta with 2 1/2 cups milk,
vegetables, thyme, and paprika in a 2-quart
saucepan. Cook over medium heat until bubbles
form around edge of milk.

In a separate bowl, dissolve cornstarch in
remaining milk. Stir cornstarch mixture into
pasta mixture and heat to simmering. Add clams
and simmer for 3 minutes, stirring frequently.
Season to taste with salt and pepper.

Avocado With Crab Salad

4 ripe avocados
8 tbsp mayonnaise, divided
1/8 tsp white pepper
1/8 tsp cayenne pepper
salt to taste
15 oz crab meat
1/2 c celery stalks, minced fine
1/4 tsp Worcestershire sauce
1 head iceberg lettuce
2 lemons, quartered

Split avocados in half lengthwise and remove
pits. Using a melon baller, gently enlarge cavity
toward stem end.

Mash avocado pulp and mix with 4 tablespoons
mayonnaise, white pepper, cayenne, and salt
to taste. Gently fold in crab meat and celery.
Divide crab mixture among 8 avocado halves.

Mix Worcestershire sauce with remaining
mayonnaise. Using a pastry bag or a cone
made from waxed paper, pipe approximately
1/2 tablespoon of mayonnaise mixture onto
each filled avocado half.

Remove outside leaves of iceberg lettuce and
arrange on a serving platter. Cut inside of lettuce
head into very thin strips and make 8 small nests
on outer leaves, lining serving platter. Place an
avocado half on each nest. Garnish with lemon
quarters.

New York Seafood Salad

1 c baby shrimp, cooked
1 c crab meat, cooked and cleaned
1 c green peas, cooked
1/2 c celery, chopped
1/2 cucumber, peeled and sliced
2 tbsp onion, minced
1/2 c Thousand Island dressing
1/4 c plain nonfat yogurt
1 tbsp prepared horseradish
1 tsp fresh lemon juice
1/4 tsp dried marjoram
1/4 tsp black pepper
lettuce leaves

In a serving bowl, combine shrimp, crab meat,
peas, celery, cucumber, and onion.

In a small bowl, combine salad dressing, yogurt,
horseradish, lemon juice, marjoram, and pepper.
Pour over salad and toss. Place a few lettuce
leaves on each of 4 serving plates. Divide salad
evenly among them and serve immediately.

South of the Border Salad

3/4 c picante sauce
2 tbsp olive oil
2 tbsp balsamic vinegar
1 tbsp red wine vinegar
1/2 tsp dried oregano
1 clove garlic, minced
1 tomato, seeded and diced
1 cucumber, sliced thin
3/4 lb deli roast beef, sliced
1 red or green bell pepper, cut into strips
1 c celery, sliced thin
1 c red onion, cut into thin strips

Combine picante sauce, oil, vinegars, oregano and garlic; mix well. Place beef in plastic bag. Pour half of picante sauce mixture into bag. Close bag securely; chill for at least 1 hour or up to 12 hours. Just before serving, arrange meat and vegetables on a serving platter. Serve with remaining dressing and additional picante sauce.

Cold Beef Salad

1 head red leaf lettuce, washed and
   torn into bite-sized pieces
1/2 sweet or red onion, sliced thin
1 carrot, sliced thin
1 c beef, cooked, chilled, and shredded
6 mushrooms, sliced thin
1/4 c cheddar, Monterey Jack, or
   Parmesan cheese, shredded
blue cheese dressing
fresh ground pepper

Toss together lettuce, onion, carrot, beef, mushrooms, and cheese. Toss with blue cheese dressing. Grind pepper over top and serve.

Grilled New York Steak Salad With Shredded Mango

10 oz tender New York steak, grilled and sliced
2 tbsp lime juice
2 tbsp fish sauce or soy sauce
1/4 tbsp garlic, chopped
1/4 tbsp lemon grass, chopped
sugar and chili pepper to taste
2 tbsp onion, sliced
2 tbsp Chinese parsley, chopped
2 tbsp carrot, sliced
2 tbsp green mango, shredded
fresh lettuce, washed and torn into pieces
fresh tomato, sliced
fresh cucumber, sliced
roasted peanuts

Toss steak with all ingredients except lettuce, tomato, cucumber, and peanuts. Serve on a bed of fresh lettuce; top with cucumber, tomato, and roasted peanuts.

Quick Oriental Cucumber Salad

1/2 c rice vinegar
1/2 tbsp brown sugar
1/2 tbsp water
1 tsp soy sauce
1 tsp sesame seeds
few drops sesame oil
1/2 cucumber, sliced thin

Combine all ingredients except cucumber in a glass jar; close tightly and shake. Chill for 1 hour. Serve over cucumber slices.

Roast Beef Salad

1 lb beef roast, cooked to medium-rare,
 then julienne-sliced
1/3 to 1/2 c walnut pieces
1/4 to 1/3 c blue cheese, crumbled
bottled herb vinaigrette dressing

Combine roast beef slices, walnut pieces,
and blue cheese. Toss with vinaigrette.

Eggplant Salad

2 large eggplants (about 1 1/4 lb each)
2 medium tomatoes, chopped
6 green onions, including tops, chopped
1 c flat-leaf parsley, minced
2 large cloves garlic, minced
2 celery stalks, chopped fine
1/4 c fresh basil, minced (or 1 tbsp
 dried leaf basil)
1/2 c red wine vinegar
1/2 tsp hot red pepper sauce
1 tsp ground cumin
1/2 tsp fresh ground black pepper
1 1/2 tsp sugar
1 tsp salt
3/4 c extra-virgin olive oil

Preheat oven to 400° F. Prick eggplants several
times with a fork and place in a baking dish.
Bake until skin is blistered and flesh is very
tender (about 45 minutes). Remove from oven;
let cool. Slice eggplants in half and scoop out
pulp. Chop pulp; discard skins.

In a medium-sized bowl, combine chopped
pulp, tomatoes, green onions, parsley, garlic,
celery, and basil. Toss to blend. Refrigerate
until chilled.

Thirty minutes before serving, combine vinegar,
pepper sauce, cumin, pepper, sugar, and salt;
whisk until blended. Whisking constantly, add
oil in a slow, steady stream. Pour dressing over
eggplant mixture; toss to combine. Let mixture
stand 30 minutes at room temperature, stirring
often. Serve.

Chicken Almond Salad

1 envelope unflavored gelatin
1/4 c cold water
1 c mayonnaise
1 c whipping cream, whipped
1 tsp salt
1 1/2 c chicken, cooked and diced
3/4 c almonds, chopped
3/4 c green seedless grapes, halved

Soften gelatin in cold water and dissolve in
top of a double boiler over hot water. Let cool
slightly. Combine with mayonnaise, cream,
and salt. Fold in chicken, almonds, and grapes.
Pour into a mold or 2-quart glass dish. Chill
until firm.

B L T Pasta Salad

1 c mayonnaise or salad dressing
1/3 c chili sauce
1/4 c lemon juice
2 tsp instant chicken bouillon
2 tsp sugar
1 pkg (7 oz) elbow macaroni,
 cooked and drained
1 large tomato, seeded and chopped
1/4 c green onions, sliced
8 slices bacon, cooked and crumbled
4 c lettuce, chopped

In large bowl combine mayonnaise, chili sauce,
lemon juice, bouillon, and sugar; stir in onions,
macaroni, and tomatoes. Cover and refrigerate.
Just before serving, stir in lettuce and bacon.

Hawaiian Turkey Salad

3 c brown rice, cooked
2 c turkey, cooked and chopped coarse
8 oz pineapple chunks in juice, drained
    (reserve juice)
8 oz water chestnuts, sliced and drained
1 medium apple, skin left on, cored, chopped
1/3 c macadamia nuts, chopped
1/2 tsp salt
1/2 c plain yogurt
lettuce leaves
1/4 c coconut, shredded and toasted

Combine rice, turkey, pineapple, water
chestnuts, apple, nuts, and salt. Toss lightly
with yogurt and 1 tablespoon reserved pineapple
juice. Serve on lettuce leaves and garnish with
coconut.

Caribbean Salad Platter

3 c watercress
3 large mangoes, pitted, peeled, and
    cut into chunks
2 cans (14 oz ea) hearts of palm, drained,
    rinsed, and sliced
2 large tomatoes, cut into large chunks
1/3 c lime juice
1/4 tsp coriander
1/4 tsp allspice
lime wedges for garnish (optional)

Arrange watercress around perimeter of a large
platter. Fill platter with alternating rows of
mango, hearts of palm, and tomatoes.

Combine lime juice, coriander, and allspice in
a small bowl. Cover and refrigerate for at least
30 minutes before serving. Garnish with lime
wedges.

Curried Apple-Raisin Salad

2 apples, cored and cubed
1 c celery, chopped
1/2 c raisins
1/2 c walnuts, chopped coarse
1/4 c mayonnaise
1/4 c sour cream
1 tbsp lemon juice
1 tsp salt
1/4 tsp curry powder
lettuce leaves

Combine apples, celery, raisins, and walnuts;
toss lightly to mix. Combine mayonnaise, sour
cream, lemon juice, salt, and curry powder,
mixing well. Pour over apple mixture and stir
gently, coating apples thoroughly. Serve over
lettuce leaves.

Warm Potato and
Tuna Salad

8 oz small new potatoes, scrubbed
3 green onions, trimmed and chopped fine
1 tbsp fresh parsley, chopped
1 tsp lemon juice
2 tsp tarragon or cider vinegar
1 tsp olive oil
2 oz tuna chunks in brine, drained
sea salt
black pepper
lemon wedges to garnish

Cook potatoes in lightly salted water for about
15 minutes or until tender. Meanwhile, mix
together onions, most of parsley, lemon juice,
vinegar, and olive oil. Drain potatoes and place
in a serving bowl. Add dressing to potatoes and
toss well. Mix tuna gently to avoid breaking.
Season with sea salt and black pepper; sprinkle
with remaining parsley. Garnish with lemon
wedges and serve while still warm.

Asparagus and Shiitake Mushroom Soup

1 lb fresh asparagus
1/2 lb shiitake mushrooms
1 tbsp vegetable oil
1 tbsp water
4 celery stalks, chopped
2 medium leeks (white part only), chopped
1 medium onion, chopped
salt
pepper
6 c chicken stock
7 tbsp unsalted butter
3/4 c flour
1 c heavy cream

Snap woody stem off each stalk of asparagus, and lightly peel half of number of stalks. Chop ends and remaining unpeeled asparagus into 1/4-inch pieces. Cover with plastic wrap and refrigerate until needed.

Blanch peeled asparagus in 3 quarts boiling salted water. Do not overcook; asparagus should remain crisp. Transfer blanched asparagus to ice water. When cool, cut into 3/4-inch pieces. Cover with plastic wrap and refrigerate until needed.

Remove and chop mushroom stems. Slice and remove caps.

Heat vegetable oil and water in a 2 1/2-quart saucepan over medium heat. When hot, add chopped asparagus, mushroom stems, celery, leeks, and onion. Season with salt and pepper and sauté until onions are translucent (about 5-7 minutes). Add chicken stock and bring to a boil.

Meanwhile, melt butter in a separate 2 1/2-quart saucepan over low heat. Add flour to make a roux; cook, stirring constantly, until roux bubbles (about 6-8 minutes). Strain 4 cups boiling stock into roux and whisk vigorously until smooth.

Add remaining stock and vegetables. Whisk until well combined. Reduce heat and simmer for 10 minutes. Remove soup from heat and purée in a food processor fitted with a metal blade.

Strain into a 5-quart saucepan and return to low heat. Hold at a simmer while completing recipe.

Heat cream, sliced mushroom caps, and blanched asparagus pieces in a nonstick sauté pan over medium heat. When hot, add to soup and season to taste. Serve immediately. (Soup may be kept hot in a double boiler for up to 1 hour.)

Curried Turkey Soup

6 c turkey stock
1 c apples, peeled and chopped
1 large onion, chopped
1/2 tsp salt
2 tsp curry powder
1/4 tsp garlic powder
1 c buttermilk
1 c turkey, cooked and diced

Simmer stock, apples, onion, salt, and curry powder for 30 minutes; purée in blender. Add garlic powder, buttermilk, and meat. Heat to just boiling, but do not allow to come to a full boil. Serve warm.

French Canadian Pea Soup

1 lb dried peas
8 c water
1/4 c fresh parsley, chopped
1 piece (1/2 lb) salt pork
1 large onion, chopped
1/2 c celery, chopped
1/4 c carrot, grated
1 small bay leaf
1 tsp dried savory
salt and pepper

Wash and sort peas; soak in cold water overnight. Drain and place in a large pot; add water, parsley, salt pork, onion, celery, carrot, bay leaf, savory, and 1 teaspoon salt. Bring to a boil; reduce heat and simmer until peas are very tender, about 2 hours, adding more water if needed. Remove salt pork; chop and return to soup. Remove and discard bay leaf. Season to taste with salt and pepper.

Cream of Crab Soup

1 chicken bouillon cube
1 c boiling water
1/4 c onion, chopped
1 c butter
3 tbsp flour
1/4 tsp celery salt
dash pepper
1 quart milk
1 lb crab meat
parsley, chopped

Dissolve bouillon cube in boiling water. Cook onion in butter until tender; blend in flour and seasonings. Add milk and bouillon gradually; cook until thickened, stirring constantly. Add crab meat and heat through. Garnish with parsley and serve.

Potato Soup

3 c red potatoes, peeled and sliced
1 c celery, chopped
1 c carrots, chopped
2 cans (14 1/2 oz) defatted chicken broth
4 oz processed American cheese
2 c evaporated skim milk
2 tbsp white wine
1/2 tsp white pepper
1/2 tsp light creole seasoning
1/2 c parsley, chopped
1/2 c green onions, chopped

In a large pot, cook potatoes, celery, and carrots in chicken broth until tender. Mash vegetables coarsely with a potato masher or a fork. Add cheese and stir over medium heat until melted. Add milk and stir again. Do not boil. Add wine, pepper, and creole seasoning; adjust if necessary. Just before serving, garnish with parsley and green onions.

Mexican Bean Soup

1/2 lb ground beef
1 medium onion, chopped
1 can (14 1/2 oz) whole tomatoes, chopped
1 can (15 oz) red kidney beans
1 can (7 oz) whole kernel corn
1 can (8 oz) tomato sauce
2 tsp chili powder
1 1/2 c water
tortilla chips, crushed, for topping (optional)

In large saucepan, brown beef with onion. Stir in remaining ingredients and simmer for about 30 minutes. Serve topped with crushed tortilla chips.

VARIATION: For a spicier soup, add 1/2 teaspoon cumin and a dash or two of hot red pepper sauce.

Cabbage Soup

1/2 c butter
2 c cabbage, chopped
1 c onion, sliced
1 c celery, sliced
1 c frozen peas, thawed
1 c carrot, sliced thin
1 can (16 oz) cream-style corn
3 c milk
1 tsp salt
1/4 tsp pepper
1 tsp dried thyme
1/4 tsp garlic powder
2 c cheddar cheese, shredded

In a large soup pot, melt butter; sauté cabbage, onion, celery, peas, and carrot until tender, about 8-10 minutes. Add corn, milk, salt, pepper, thyme, and garlic powder; simmer for about 15 minutes. Add cheese and stir until melted. Serve.

Tortilla Soup

2 tsp olive oil
1/3 c onion, diced
1 tsp garlic, minced
1 jalapeño pepper, seeded and minced
8 c canned rich chicken stock
1 c fresh tomatoes, diced
1/2 c tomato juice
2 tbsp chili powder
1 tbsp cumin
2 tsp oregano
2 tsp cilantro, chopped
corn chips, crushed
Monterey Jack cheese, grated

Sauté first 4 ingredients in a large saucepan until onions become transparent. Add next 6 ingredients and heat to a boil.

Reduce heat and simmer for 30 minutes. Add cilantro and simmer for 5 minutes more. To serve, place 2 tablespoons crushed corn tortilla chips in individual serving bowls. Ladle in soup and top with 1 tablespoon shredded cheese.

Zucchini Stew

1/2 lb ground beef
1 onion, chopped
1/3 c olive oil
1 small green pepper
2 tsp salt
1/2 tsp basil
2 celery stalks, chopped fine
1 clove garlic, minced
2 lb zucchini, cut into 1/4-inch slices
2 medium potatoes, sliced thin
1 tbsp tomato paste
1 1/2 c water

Brown ground beef and onion lightly in a 4-quart kettle. Add remaining ingredients; cover and simmer for 30-40 minutes or until zucchini is tender. Do not overcook. Serve with crusty Italian bread.

Cowboy Soup

1 lb ground beef, browned and drained
1 medium onion
1 can (16 oz) mixed vegetables
1 can (10 oz) tomatoes with green chilies
1 can (13 oz) Spanish rice
1 can (14 1/2 oz) stewed tomatoes
1 can (17 oz) cream-style corn

Combine all ingredients in a 4-quart kettle and heat through.

One-Dish Meals

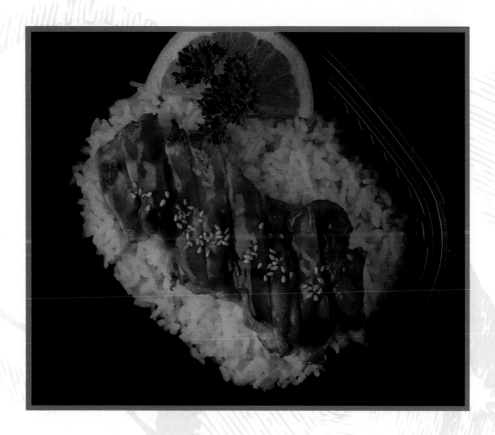

Broil:
To cook food directly above or under a heat source, in an oven or a grill.

Chop:
To cut into small, irregular-shaped pieces.

Linguine Alfredo

1 can (14 oz) chicken broth
1/4 c all-purpose flour
1/4 tsp garlic powder
1/4 tsp pepper
1/3 c plain yogurt
6 c linguine, cooked without salt
6 tbsp Parmesan cheese, grated
fresh parsley, chopped

In medium saucepan mix broth, flour, garlic powder, and pepper until smooth. Simmer over medium heat until mixture boils and thickens, stirring constantly. Remove from heat and stir in yogurt. Toss with hot pasta and 4 tablespoons cheese. Sprinkle with parsley and remaining cheese.

Light Vegetable Pasta

3/4 c frozen corn
3/4 c kidney beans, cooked
1/2 c spaghetti sauce
1/4 tsp chili powder
salt and pepper to taste
4 oz rigatoni, cooked and drained

Stir all ingredients except pasta in a small saucepan and cook until heated through. Add pasta and mix well.

Spicy Cabbage

1 tsp vegetable oil
2 oz cooked smoked ham, chopped
1/2 c onion, chopped
1/2 c green bell pepper, chopped
1 can (10 oz) tomatoes with green chilies, diced
1/2 tsp sugar
4 c cabbage, sliced
1/4 tsp black pepper
1/4 tsp hot red pepper sauce

Heat oil in large skillet on medium heat. Stir in ham, onion, and green pepper and cook until vegetables are tender-crisp. Add tomatoes and sugar; simmer for 3 minutes. Add cabbage, black pepper, and red pepper sauce. Simmer 15 minutes, stirring occasionally.

Stuffed Tomatoes

6 medium tomatoes
2 tbsp vegetable oil
1/4 c celery, chopped
2 tbsp onion, chopped
2 c brown rice, cooked
1/4 c Parmesan cheese, grated
1 tbsp fresh parsley, snipped
1 tsp dried basil leaves, crushed
1/4 tsp black pepper
1/4 tsp garlic powder

Preheat oven to 350° F. Cut one thin slice from top of each tomato; set aside. Scoop out centers of tomatoes. Chop pulp and reserve. Place tomato shells upside down on paper towels to drain.

Heat oil in medium saucepan; add celery and onion. Cook over medium heat until tender. Remove from heat and add reserved pulp, rice, Parmesan cheese, parsley, basil, pepper, and garlic powder.

Mix well and fill each tomato shell evenly with mixture. Replace tomato tops. Lightly spray round baking dish with cooking spray. Place tomatoes in dish and cover with foil. Bake for 30-45 minutes or until tomatoes are tender.

Zucchini Boats

3 medium zucchini, cut in half lengthwise
1 small onion, chopped fine
1 medium clove garlic, minced
1/4 tsp ground nutmeg
2 tbsp margarine
1 1/2 c fresh spinach, chopped
1/2 c ricotta cheese
juice and zest of 1/2 lemon
2 tbsp Parmesan cheese, grated

Boil zucchini in water for 5 minutes; drain. Preheat oven to 375° F. In large skillet over medium-high heat, cook and stir onion, garlic, and nutmeg in margarine until onion is tender. Add spinach, ricotta cheese, lemon zest, and lemon juice, mixing thoroughly. Arrange zucchini, cut sides up, in a shallow baking dish. Top zucchini halves evenly with spinach mixture. Bake for 20 minutes. Sprinkle with Parmesan cheese before serving.

Cheesy Ziti and Vegetables

8 oz ziti
1 1/2 tbsp vegetable oil
2 scallions, chopped fine
1/2 tsp Italian seasoning
2 tbsp horseradish
1/2 c skim milk
4 oz (1 c) cheddar cheese, grated
1 1/2 c mixed vegetables, cooked
salt and fresh ground black pepper to taste

Prepare pasta according to package directions; drain. Meanwhile, heat oil in a medium saucepan. Add scallions and sauté over medium heat until limp but not brown. Remove from heat. Stir in Italian seasoning, horseradish, milk, and cheese. Cook over medium heat until thickened. Stir in cooked vegetables until warm. Place pasta in a large bowl and toss with sauce.

Creamy Ham Penne

1 lb ziti, uncooked
1/2 tsp vegetable oil
12 oz lean turkey ham, cut into bite-sized pieces
1 c red pepper, diced
1 c nonfat sour cream
1 pkg (10-oz) frozen spinach,
  thawed and drained well
3/4 c skim milk
1/4 c Dijon mustard
1/4 c fresh parsley, chopped
2 tbsp fresh dill, minced
1 tbsp lemon juice
3/4 tsp hot sauce
salt and pepper to taste

Prepare pasta according to package directions; drain well. Meanwhile, warm oil in a large skillet over medium heat. Add ham and red pepper and cook until browned. Purée sour cream, spinach, milk, mustard, parsley, dill, lemon juice, and hot sauce in a blender until very smooth. Add purée to ham and simmer. Toss warm pasta with sauce. Season with salt and pepper and serve.

Turkey Pie

1 lb ground turkey
1 c salsa
1 can refrigerated crescent rolls
1/4 c sharp cheddar cheese, shredded

Preheat oven to 450° F. Cook turkey in nonstick skillet over medium heat until browned. Stir frequently to break turkey into small pieces. Stir in salsa and heat through. Meanwhile, line a 9-inch pie plate with crescent roll dough, pressing evenly on bottom, sides, and rim of dish. Spread turkey mixture evenly over crust and sprinkle with cheddar cheese. Bake 18-20 minutes or until crust is browned.

Spaghetti Carbonara

1 lb spaghetti, uncooked
6 oz turkey bacon, chopped fine
3 cloves garlic, minced
2/3 c dry white wine
1 c egg substitute
1/3 c parsley, chopped
1/3 c Parmesan cheese, grated
salt and fresh ground pepper to taste

Prepare pasta according to package directions. While pasta is cooking, cook bacon and garlic in a small skillet over medium-low heat until garlic is aromatic and bacon is lightly browned, about 3-4 minutes. Stir in wine and increase heat, bringing mix to a boil. Cook until wine is reduced by about half. Pour mixture into a large serving bowl and let it cool for 5 minutes. Stir in egg substitute and parsley. Drain cooked pasta; add immediately to bacon mixture. Add Parmesan cheese and toss quickly. Season with salt and fresh ground pepper and serve.

Pineapple Chicken and Pasta

8 oz mostaccioli
1 lb boneless and skinless chicken breasts
1/8 tsp cayenne pepper
2 bunches scallions, cut into 1-inch diagonals
1 1/2 c pineapple juice
1 tbsp fresh ginger, grated
1 tbsp honey
1 tbsp lemon juice
1 tbsp butter
1 can mandarin oranges, drained

Preheat oven to 350° F. Brush chicken with oil and season with cayenne pepper. Bake until cooked through, about 30 minutes.

During the last 2 to 3 minutes of cooking, add scallions to pan. Cool and cut chicken into bite-sized pieces. Reserve scallions.

Prepare pasta according to package directions. Meanwhile, combine pineapple juice, ginger, and honey in a small saucepan. Bring to a boil over medium-high heat and cook until reduced by half, about 20 minutes. Add lemon juice. Remove from heat and whisk in butter. Toss together pasta, chicken, scallions, mandarin oranges, and sauce.

Pork and Broccoli Stir-Fry

1 can (14 1/2 oz) chicken broth
2 tbsp cornstarch
1 tbsp soy sauce
4 green onions, chopped fine
1 lb pork tenderloin
1 tbsp vegetable oil
1 clove garlic, minced
1 1/2 lb fresh broccoli
2 tbsp pimento, sliced
2 tbsp sesame seed, lightly toasted

Combine chicken broth, cornstarch, and soy sauce in small bowl. Stir in green onions and set aside.

Cut pork tenderloin lengthwise into quarters, cutting each quarter into bite-sized pieces. Heat oil in wok over medium high heat. Add pork and garlic; stir-fry for 3-4 minutes or until pork is tender. Remove pork and keep warm.

Add broth mixture and broccoli to wok. Cover and simmer over low heat for 8 minutes. Add cooked pork and pimento. Cook just until mixture is hot, stirring frequently. Sprinkle with sesame seed and serve.

24

Vegetable Lasagna

9 pieces lasagna
1 c yellow onion, chopped
1 tsp vegetable oil
2 cloves garlic, crushed
8 oz mushrooms, sliced thin
1/4 c fresh parsley, chopped
1/4 tsp salt
1 pkg (10-oz) frozen spinach,
  thawed and drained
1/2 tsp dried oregano
1/2 tsp dried basil
2 c spaghetti sauce, divided
15 oz reduced-fat ricotta cheese
3/4 c part-skim mozzarella cheese, shredded
2 tbsp Parmesan cheese, grated

Preheat oven to 350° F. Prepare pasta according to package directions; drain and cover with cool water until ready to use.

Sauté onions in oil over medium heat until golden, about 5 minutes. Add garlic and cook about 1 minute. Spoon out half of onions and reserve. Add mushrooms to onions in skillet. Cook about 7 minutes over medium heat, stirring constantly, until mushrooms are tender and slightly browned. Add parsley and a pinch of salt; transfer to a bowl.

Add reserved cooked onion and spinach to skillet. Cover and cook over medium heat until spinach is wilted, about 3 minutes. Uncover and cook over medium heat to evaporate any excess moisture, about 1 minute. Season with a pinch of salt.

Drain lasagna and pat dry with paper towels. Mix oregano and basil with tomato sauce. Spread bottom of a 13x9x3-inch pan with 1 cup tomato sauce. Arrange 3 lasagna pieces in pan.

(They will overlap slightly.) Spoon spinach mixture evenly over top. Spread with half of ricotta. Sprinkle with 1/4 cup shredded mozzarella. Arrange a layer of 3 more lasagna pieces. Spread with mushrooms, remaining ricotta mixture, and 1/4 cup mozzarella. Top with remaining 3 pieces of lasagna, 1 cup of tomato sauce and 1/2 cup mozzarella cheese. Sprinkle with Parmesan cheese. Bake until brown and bubbly, about 45 minutes.

Chicken Fajitas

1 tbsp vegetable oil
1 large green bell pepper, sliced thin
1 large red pepper, sliced thin
1 large onion, sliced thin
1 clove garlic, minced
4 boneless and skinless chicken breast
  halves, cut into 1/2-inch strips
1/2 tsp oregano
2 tbsp water
salt and pepper to taste
12 flour tortillas

Heat oil in large skillet over medium heat. Add peppers, onion, and garlic; stir-fry for 3-4 minutes. Remove vegetables with slotted spoon and set aside.

Add chicken and oregano to skillet. Cook 4 minutes or until chicken is no longer pink, stirring occasionally. Return vegetables to skillet and add water. Season with salt and pepper; cover. Continue cooking 2 minutes or until thoroughly heated. Warm tortillas according to package directions. Fill warmed tortillas with chicken mixture. Serve with sour cream or guacamole, if desired.

Turkey Quiche

3 c rice, cooked and cooled
1 1/2 c turkey, cooked and chopped
1 medium tomato, seeded and diced fine
1/4 c green onion, sliced
1/4 c green bell pepper, diced fine
1 tsp dried basil
1/2 tsp salt
1/4 tsp ground red pepper
1/2 c skim milk
3 eggs, beaten
1/2 c cheddar cheese, shredded
1/2 c mozzarella cheese, shredded

Preheat oven to 375° F. Combine rice, turkey, tomato, onion, green pepper, basil, salt, red pepper, milk, and eggs in a 13x9-inch pan coated with cooking spray. Top with cheeses. Bake for 20 minutes or until knife inserted in center comes out clean.

Turkey Sloppy Joes

1 lb ground turkey
1 c onion, sliced thin
1/2 c green bell pepper, chopped
1 c ketchup
1/4 c sweet pickle relish
1 1/2 tsp chili powder
1 tsp Worchestershire sauce
1/2 tsp salt
1/2 tsp garlic powder
8 hard rolls

In large skillet over medium-high heat, cook and stir turkey, onion, and bell pepper for 5 minutes or until turkey is no longer pink; drain. Add ketchup, relish, chili powder, Worchestershire sauce, salt, and garlic powder. Bring to a boil.

Reduce heat to low; cover and simmer for 30 minutes. Slice rolls in half and toast under broiler for 1-2 minutes or until lightly browned.

Serve by spooning turkey mixture onto bottom halves of rolls.

Chicken Spinach Casserole

1 broiler fryer chicken, cooked, skinned, and chopped
1 pkg (10 oz) frozen spinach
1/4 c onion, chopped fine
1/2 tsp garlic powder, divided
1 c fresh mushrooms, sliced
2 tbsp light margarine, melted
1 c low-fat mozzarella cheese

Preheat oven to 350° F. Cook spinach according to package instructions, omitting salt; drain well.

Mix onion with spinach.

Arrange spinach mixture in bottom of a 1 1/2-quart baking dish; sprinkle with 1/4 teaspoon garlic powder.

Arrange mushrooms on spinach and drizzle with melted margarine. Place chicken on mushrooms and sprinkle with remaining garlic powder.

Top with mozzarella cheese. Bake 30 minutes and serve.

Light Turkey Jambalaya

1 tbsp olive oil

1 onion, chopped fine

1 green bell pepper, stemmed, seeded,
and chopped coarse

1 red bell pepper, stemmed, seeded,
and chopped coarse

2 cloves garlic, peeled and minced

2 cans (14 1/2 oz ea) diced tomatoes in purée

1 can (14 1/2 oz) low-sodium chicken broth

1 tsp paprika

1/2 tsp onion powder

1/2 tsp garlic powder

1/2 tsp dried thyme leaves, crushed

1/2 tsp ground cumin

1 1/2 lb turkey breast with bone, skin removed

1/2 lb turkey sausage, cut into 1/4-inch slices

1 c white rice

1/4 tsp hot sauce

1/4 tsp salt

1/4 tsp fresh ground black pepper

Heat olive oil in a large pot over medium heat.
Add onion and bell peppers; sauté 5 minutes.
Add garlic and sauté 2 minutes more.

Add tomatoes, broth, paprika, onion powder,
garlic powder, thyme and cumin; bring to a boil.
Reduce heat and simmer 10 minutes. Add turkey
breast to pot. Cover and simmer for 45 minutes
until cooked through. Remove turkey from pot
and allow it to cool slightly. Add sausage and
rice to pot. Cover and cook over medium-low
heat for 15 minutes, stirring occasionally.

Dice cooled turkey and add it back to pot. Add
hot sauce, salt, and pepper. Cook on medium-
low heat for 10 minutes or until sausage is
cooked through.

Lone Star Chicken Casserole

2 whole chickens, cut up

2 c flour

salt, pepper, and ginger to taste

4 tbsp butter, melted

2 tbsp flour

1 c water

1 can (10-3/4 oz) beef broth

1 tbsp ketchup

1 tbsp Worcestershire sauce

2 bay leaves

6 onions, peeled and quartered

6 potatoes, peeled and quartered

6 carrots, peeled and quartered

8 oz mushrooms

1 can (8 oz) green peas

Mix 2 cups flour, salt, pepper, and ginger;
dredge chicken pieces in seasoned flour.

Brown floured chicken in a skillet with butter.
Remove chicken pieces, reserving drippings.

Arrange chicken pieces in a large casserole.
Add flour to drippings, making a paste.

Stir in water, beef broth, ketchup,
Worcestershire sauce, bay leaves, and onions.
Pour over chicken and bake at 350° F for
45 minutes.

Add potatoes, carrots, and mushrooms.
Bake 35 minutes more. Add peas and bake
an additional 10 minutes.

Nacho Chicken Casserole

2 c plain tortilla chips, crushed
2 c chicken, cooked and diced
2 c cream of mushroom soup
4 oz sour cream
1 c picante sauce
1 c cheddar cheese, shredded

Line bottom of casserole with crushed tortilla chips. Mix all remaining ingredients except cheese; pour over chips. Top with cheese. Bake at 350° F until cheese is bubbly. Serve with spicy salsa.

Light Broil With Vegetables

1/2 c light soy sauce
2 tbsp honey
2 tbsp lemon juice
2 green onions, chopped fine
1/4 tsp garlic powder
1 lb beef top round or boneless sirloin,
    cut into 1-inch slices
6 oz asparagus tips, blanched
3/4 c carrots, blanched
1/2 c frozen peas, blanched

Combine soy sauce, honey, lemon juice, onions, and garlic powder. Pour over beef, turning to coat. Marinate in refrigerator for 6-8 hours, turning occasionally. Pour off and discard marinade.

Broil steak 3-4 inches from heat, 16-20 minutes for medium-rare, turning once. Keep steak warm. Meanwhile, arrange an equal amount of each vegetable, in spoke fashion, on 4 dinner plates. Carve steak into 1/4-inch thick slices. Arrange 4 slices of beef over vegetables.

Seafood Rice Casserole

1/2 c onion, chopped
1/4 c bell pepper, chopped
1/2 c butter
water
4 c chicken broth
1/4 tsp garlic, minced
1 tbsp celery, chopped
parsley, chopped
salt to taste
MSG
2 c mushrooms, sliced
2 cans clams
2 c rice
1/2 vial saffron, shredded
1 lb scallops
1 lb shrimp, peeled and deveined
1/2 lb crab meat
black pepper to taste

Sauté onion and bell pepper in butter until translucent.

Add water, chicken broth, garlic, celery, parsley, salt, MSG, mushrooms, and clams; cover and bring to boil over medium-high heat.

When water comes to rolling boil, add rice and bring back to a low boil. Add saffron. Cover and cook for 15 minutes.

Add remaining seafood and stir thoroughly. Bring back to a simmer; cover and cook 10 minutes.

If shrimp exude a lot of liquid, uncover and continue cooking until liquid is absorbed.

Scallops and Vegetables

2 strips bacon, cut up
1/2 c onion, chopped
1/2 lb bay scallops
1/2 lb mushrooms, sliced
1/2 lb snow peas
1 tbsp dry sherry
2 tsp cornstarch
1 tbsp water
1 tbsp lemon juice
1/2 tsp salt

Brown bacon in skillet. Set aside to drain on paper towels.

Drain all but 1 tablespoon of fat from skillet. Add onion and scallops and cook until scallops are white, about 3 minutes. Remove from skillet and keep warm. Add mushrooms, snow peas, and sherry to skillet; cover and cook for 3 minutes.

Combine cornstarch and water in a small bowl; add to skillet, stirring until thickened. Stir reserved bacon, reserved scallops, lemon juice, and salt into skillet. Heat to serving temperature and serve over rice.

Turkey Loaf

1 1/2 lb ground turkey
1 1/2 c dry bread crumbs
1 c unsweetened applesauce
2 egg whites
1/4 c onion, minced
1/4 c celery, chopped fine
1 tbsp prepared mustard
1 tbsp Worchestershire sauce
1 tsp salt
1 tsp pepper
2/3 c chili sauce

Mix all ingredients except chili sauce in a large bowl; press into loaf pan. Top with chili sauce. Bake at 350° F for 1 hour or until meat is cooked through. Let stand 10 minutes before slicing.

Creamy Tuna Rice

1 c water
1/2 c milk
1/2 tsp dill weed
1/4 tsp salt
6 slices processed American cheese
1 1/2 c instant rice
1 can tuna, drained
2 tsp fresh parsley, chopped

Bring water, milk, dill, and salt to boil in medium saucepan over medium heat. Add cheese; cook and stir until cheese is melted. Stir in rice, tuna, and parsley; cover. Remove from heat. Let stand 5 minutes or until liquid is absorbed. Stir.

Crab Casserole

2 eggs, separated
1 1/2 c white sauce
1 lb crab meat
pinch parsley or green pepper
1/2 tsp hot red pepper sauce
salt and pepper to taste

Beat egg yolks and add to white sauce. Mix all ingredients and fold in egg whites. Bake at 375° F until brown, about 20 minutes.

For white sauce, melt 3 tablespoons of butter in heavy saucepan. Add 3 tablespoons of flour, 1/4 teaspoon of salt and a dash of pepper. Add 1 1/2 cups milk, stirring over medium heat until mixture thickens.

Pizza Casserole

1 jar pizza sauce
1 lb ground beef
1/2 onion, chopped
1 c water
1/2 green pepper, chopped
1 pkg pepperoni, sliced
2 c egg noodles
mozzarella cheese, grated

Layer ingredients in a casserole dish in following order: sauce, beef, onion, water, pepper, pepperoni, egg noodles.

Cover with plastic wrap and microwave for 5 minutes on high. Stir and microwave for 5 minutes more.

Sprinkle liberally with mozzarella cheese and let stand until cheese melts.

OVEN METHOD: To prepare in oven, cook noodles and omit water. Cook at 350° F until bubbly, about 40 minutes.

One-Dish Pork Chops With Rice

2 tbsp vegetable oil
1/4 c onion, chopped
3 tbsp green pepper, chopped
1 c white rice
2 tsp sugar
2 c stewed tomatoes, chopped
4 pork chops
1/2 c Parmesan cheese, grated

Preheat oven to 350° F. Heat oil in a skillet that can go into oven; add onion, green pepper, and rice.

Sauté until rice is translucent. Blend in sugar and tomatoes. Top with pork chops and then cheese.

Cover and bake for 50 minutes. Uncover and carefully stir rice mixture. Replace cover and bake about 10 minutes more.

Pork and Cashew Stir-Fry

2 tbsp vegetable oil
1 lb pork tenderloin, cut into 1/2-inch strips
2 tbsp soy sauce
2 medium carrots, sliced
1 green bell pepper, diced
1/2 c roasted and unsalted cashews
2 tbsp brown sugar
1 tbsp cornstarch
3 tbsp water
salt to taste

Heat vegetable oil in wok or heavy skillet over high heat. Add pork and stir-fry for 3-4 minutes or until lightly browned.

Add soy sauce; stir-fry 1 minute more. Reduce heat to medium and add carrots. Cover and cook 3 minutes.

Add green peppers and cashews; stir-fry 3-4 minutes. Sprinkle with brown sugar and stir until dissolved, about 1 minute.

Dissolve cornstarch in water; add to wok. Stir and cook until sauce thickens and clears. Season with salt to taste. Serve immediately.

Red Beans and Rice With Smoked Sausage

1 lb dried red beans
1 clove garlic, chopped
1 1/2 lb smoked sausage, cut into chunks
1 tsp dried thyme
1 tsp ground pepper
8 oz smoked ham shanks
1/2 tsp sage
1 large onion, chopped
pinch cayenne pepper
salt
rice, cooked and hot

Place beans in Dutch oven and cover generously with water. Let soak 30 minutes. Add all remaining ingredients except salt and rice. Bring to boil over medium-high heat. Reduce heat to medium-low; cover and simmer until beans are tender (about 2 1/2 hours), adding more water if necessary. Add salt to taste.

Discard ham bones. Remove about 3 tablespoons of beans from mixture and mash to paste; return paste to Dutch oven and stir. Simmer 15 minutes more. Serve over hot rice.

Savory Pork and Vegetables

4 boneless pork chops, each 3/4-inch thick
2 tbsp butter, divided
1 1/2 c mushrooms, sliced
1/2 tsp dried rosemary leaves, crushed
1 can (10 3/4 oz) cream of mushroom soup
2 tbsp water
1/2 lb fresh green beans, cut into 2-inch pieces *or* 9 oz. frozen cut green beans

In skillet, cook chops in 1 tablespoon butter for 10 minutes or until browned on both sides. Remove.

Cook mushrooms with rosemary and remaining butter in skillet until tender and liquid is evaporated, stirring often.

Add soup, water, and green beans. Heat to boiling. Return chops to skillet; cover. Cook over low heat, stirring occasionally, for 10 minutes or until chops are no longer pink and green beans are tender. Serve with fettuccine, if desired.

Mexican Chicken Noodle Casserole

3/4 c celery, chopped
2 green pepper rings, chopped
3/4 c onion, chopped
1/2 tsp butter
1 pkg flour tortillas, cut into strips
1 can cream of chicken soup
2/3 c milk
1/2 c sour cream
2 c cheddar cheese, shredded
1/2 pkg noodles, cooked
2 c chicken, cooked and chopped
1/2 lb mushrooms, sliced
1 tbsp jalepeños, minced
1/2 c sliced almonds

Combine celery, pepper rings, onion, and butter in a microwave casserole dish. Microwave 2 minutes. Remove from dish. Line casserole with tortilla strips. In another bowl, stir together soup, milk, sour cream, and cheese. Add cooked vegetables, noodles, chicken, mushrooms, and jalepeños. Pour into casserole. Top with almonds. Cook in microwave until heated through, about 2-4 minutes.

Reuben Casserole

1 c sauerkraut, rinsed and drained
1 c corned beef, chopped
2 c Swiss cheese, shredded
1/2 c mayonnaise
1/4 c Thousand Island dressing
2 tomatoes, sliced *or* 1 green pepper,
  cut into rings
2 tsp butter
1/4 c bread crumbs

Spray a 1 1/2-quart casserole with cooking
spray. Add sauerkraut, corned beef, then cheese.
Combine mayonnaise and Thousand Island
dressing; spread over cheese. Top with tomatoes
or green pepper. Melt butter and blend with
bread crumbs; spread over top. Microwave on
high for 12 minutes.

Potato and Egg Casserole

4 medium-sized potatoes, peeled and sliced thin
1 tsp salt
1/4 tsp pepper
1/4 tsp nutmeg
3 tbsp olive oil
1/2 c American cheese, grated
4 eggs
3/4 c evaporated milk

Preheat oven to 350° F. Sprinkle potatoes with
salt, pepper, and nutmeg. Heat olive oil in a
skillet; cook potatoes in olive oil until browned
and tender, stirring frequently.

Spread potatoes evenly in a greased 1-quart
casserole; sprinkle with cheese. Break eggs
carefully over cheese; cover with evaporated
milk. Bake for 15-20 minutes or until eggs are
set. Serve at once.

Potato-Cabbage Casserole

1 1/2 lb Idaho potatoes, unpeeled
water
1/2 lb bacon, cut into 3-inch strips
1 c onion, sliced
2 tbsp flour
1/2 tsp thyme, dried
1/2 tsp salt
1 1/2 c (12 oz) beer
1/2 c milk
6 c (1.5 lb) cabbage, shredded fine
1 c Swiss cheese, shredded

Preheat oven to 350° F. Steam potatoes in 1 inch
boiling water for 30-40 minutes or until tender.
Slice unpeeled potatoes into 1/2-inch slices; set
aside.

Cook bacon in a large skillet until crisp; set
aside. Pour off all but 2 tablespoons bacon fat;
add onion and sauté until golden.

Stir in flour, thyme, and salt. Gradually add beer
and milk; cook over low heat, stirring
constantly, until mixture boils and thickens.

In a 3-quart casserole, layer half of cabbage,
potatoes, bacon, cheese, and sauce; repeat with
remaining ingredients.

Cover and bake for 30 minutes. Uncover and
bake 15 minutes longer, or until cabbage is
tender.

Mexican Quiche

4 oz green chilies, drained and chopped
6 slices bacon, cooked and crumbled
5 eggs
2 c light cream
1/4 tsp salt
4 taco shells
1 c Swiss cheese, shredded
cayenne pepper

Mix bacon and chilies. Beat together eggs, cream, and salt. Pour ingredients into shells in following order: cheese, bacon-chili mixture, and egg mixture. Sprinkle with cayenne pepper. Bake at 350° F for 25-30 minutes. Cool 5 minutes.

Spaghetti With Shrimp and Mushrooms

1/2 lb spaghetti
1 egg
1/2 c half-and-half *or* light cream
1/2 c Parmesan cheese, grated
1/2 tsp dry mustard
1/4 c parsley, chopped (optional)
4 tsp anchovy paste or 4 flat anchovies, minced (optional)
1/4 tsp pepper
3 tsp olive oil, divided
2 cloves garlic, crushed
1/4 lb mushrooms, sliced
3/4 lb medium shrimp, shelled and deveined
1 bunch (6 to 8) scallions, chopped coarse

Cook pasta in 4 quarts boiling water until *al dente*, about 10 to 12 minutes. While pasta is cooking, beat egg. Stir in cream, cheese, mustard, parsley (if using), anchovy paste (if using), and pepper; set aside. In a large skillet, warm 2 tablespoons oil over medium-high heat until hot but not smoking. Add garlic and mushrooms. Stir-fry until mushrooms are almost limp, about 5 minutes. Add remaining oil and shrimp; stir-fry for 2 minutes. Add scallions and stir-fry for 1-2 minutes longer or until shrimp turn pink and opaque. Place a colander over a large serving bowl. Drain pasta into colander, letting boiling water heat serving bowl. Pour water out of bowl and add hot pasta. Pour beaten egg mixture over hot pasta and toss to cook eggs and coat pasta. Add shrimp-vegetable mixture and toss to distribute evenly. Serve hot.

Mexican Corn Lasagna

1 lb ground beef
1 can (17 oz) whole kernel corn, drained
1 can (15 oz) tomato sauce
1 c picante sauce
1 tbsp chili powder
1 1/2 tsp ground cumin
1 carton (16 oz) low-fat cottage cheese
2 eggs, slightly beaten
1/4 c Parmesan cheese
1 tsp dried oregano
1/2 tsp garlic salt
12 corn tortillas
1 c (4 oz) cheddar cheese, shredded

Preheat oven to 375° F. Brown meat; drain. Add corn, tomato sauce, picante sauce, chili powder, and cumin. Simmer for 5 minutes, stirring frequently. Combine cottage cheese, eggs, Parmesan, oregano, and garlic salt. Mix well.

Arrange 6 tortillas on bottom and sides of lightly greased 13x9x2-inch baking dish, overlapping as necessary. Top with half of meat mixture. Spoon cheese mixture over meat. Arrange remaining 6 tortillas over cheese. Top with remaining meat mixture. Bake for 30 minutes. Remove from oven; top with cheddar cheese. Let stand 10 minutes before serving.

Spicy Cold Noodles With Chicken

1/2 lb thin Chinese flour noodles
2 tbsp peanut oil
1 medium chicken breast
2 green onions, slivered
3 egg yolks
1 tsp cool water
1 tbsp thin soy sauce
1 tsp Chinkiang vinegar
1 tsp hot chili pepper oil
1/2 tsp ginger juice
1 clove garlic, minced
1 pinch sugar
2 tbsp oil

Cook noodles in boiling, salted water until chewy; rinse in cold water and drain. Toss noodles with 1/2 teaspoon peanut oil to prevent sticking. Cover and refrigerate until ready to use.

Remove and discard skin from chicken breast. Steam breast for 15 minutes; remove from steamer and cool uncovered. Shred chicken with fingers into 3-inch strips.

Mix yolks with cool water. Place skillet over medium heat and brush with remaining peanut oil. Pour some egg yolk mixture into skillet; spread to make a thin sheet; remove when egg is set. Repeat until egg is used. Cool egg sheets. Slice into thin strips to match chicken shreds.

Mix soy sauce, vinegar, chili oil, ginger juice, garlic, and sugar. Heat oil until it begins to smoke; add to other ingredients. Cool. Mix dressing with cold noodles, chicken, and onion. Garnish with egg strips. Serve immediately.

Linguine Tuna Salad

7 oz linguine, broken in half
1/4 c lemon juice
1/4 c vegetable oil
1/4 c green onion, chopped
2 tsp sugar
1 tsp Italian seasoning
1 tsp seasoned salt
1 can (12 1/2 oz) tuna, drained
1 pkg (10 oz) frozen green peas, thawed
2 medium-sized firm tomatoes, chopped

Cook linguine according to package directions, drain. In a large bowl, combine lemon juice, oil, onion, sugar, Italian seasoning, and salt; mix well. Add hot linguine; toss. Add remaining ingredients; mix well. Cover; chill to blend flavors. Serve on lettuce leaves and garnish as desired.

Pasta Salad With Chicken and Artichokes

1 lb pasta shells
2 tbsp oil
1 1/2 c mayonnaise
3 tbsp lemon juice
3 tbsp fresh parsley, chopped *or* 1 tsp
  dried parsley
3 c chicken, cooked and diced
1 jar (6 oz) artichokes, chopped and drained
dash hot red pepper sauce
toasted almonds

Cook pasta according to package directions. Drain well and rinse with cold water. Shake out excess water and toss pasta with oil. Place pasta in large bowl.

Combine mayonnaise, lemon juice, parsley, and basil. Add mayonnaise mixture, chicken, artichokes, and pepper sauce to pasta; toss well. Garnish with almonds.

34

Sparerib, Rice, and Chick-Pea Casserole

2 1/2 lb country-style spareribs
salt and pepper
1 large onion, chopped
4 large cloves garlic, chopped
2 cans (14 1/2 oz) beef broth
2 c long-grain white rice
1 can (16 oz) chick-peas
    (garbanzo beans), drained
2/3 c water
1/3 c red wine vinegar
2 tbsp chopped fresh cilantro
1 tbsp paprika
1 tbsp dried oregano, crumbled
1 jar (4 oz) pimientos, drained and sliced

Preheat oven to 350° F. Season spareribs with salt and pepper. Brown spareribs in large heavy Dutch oven over high heat; transfer to plate and set aside.

Add onion and garlic to pot; sauté until onion is translucent, about 5 minutes. Add all remaining ingredients except pimientos and bring to a boil, scraping up browned bits. Return ribs and their juices to pot. Push ribs into rice mixture. Season with salt and pepper. Spread pimientos evenly over top. Cover and bake until meat and rice are tender and all liquids are absorbed (about 50 minutes).

Turkey Casserole With Rice

2 medium onions, chopped
2 tbsp butter, divided
1/2 lb sliced mushrooms
2 c cold turkey, diced
1/2 c ham, diced
1 c leftover stuffing, crumbled
2 tbsp parsley, chopped

pinch of thyme
salt and fresh ground black pepper to taste
1 tbsp curry powder
1 c rice
2 c turkey *or* chicken broth, heated

Preheat oven to 375° F. Sauté onions in 1 tablespoon butter until just tender. Add mushrooms; sauté for 2 minutes. In a 2-quart casserole combine mushrooms, onions, turkey, ham, stuffing, parsley, thyme, salt, and pepper.

Add remaining butter and curry powder to skillet; sauté rice. Add sautéed rice and hot broth to casserole. Bake until rice is tender and liquid is absorbed. If needed, add more hot broth to finish cooking rice.

French Toast With Banana-Orange Filling

1/2 c plain low-fat yogurt
2 tbsp pure maple syrup
1 medium-sized ripe banana
2 tsp frozen orange juice concentrate, thawed
4 slices cinnamon raisin bread
2 egg whites
1/4 c low-fat milk
1 tablespoon butter

Whisk yogurt and maple syrup to blend in small bowl. Set aside.

Combine banana and orange concentrate in medium bowl. Using a fork, mash to a coarse paste. Spread banana mixture on 2 slices of bread. Top with remaining slices bread, pressing to adhere. Blend egg whites and milk in a shallow bowl. Melt butter in large nonstick skillet over medium heat. Dip both sides of each sandwich briefly into milk mixture. Cook until brown, about 3 minutes per side. Transfer to plates and serve with maple yogurt.

Mexican Chicken and Vegetable Casserole

3 cloves garlic, minced
salt
1 tsp ground cumin
1 tsp chili powder
1/2 tsp cinnamon
2 tsp white wine vinegar
3 tablespoons vegetable oil, divided
pepper
8 chicken thighs (about 2 lb)
1 large onion, sliced thin
2 tomatoes, chopped coarse
4 zucchini (about 1 1/2 lb), scrubbed, quartered
   lengthwise, and cut crosswise into
   3/4-inch pieces
1/4 c chicken broth
2 tbsp pickled jalapeño pepper, drained
   and minced (wear rubber gloves)
1 red bell pepper, cut into 1/2-inch pieces
1 c fresh corn or frozen corn, thawed
1/4 tsp dried orégano, crumbled
1/2 c Monterey Jack, grated coarse

Mash 1 clove garlic to a paste with a pinch of salt. In a small bowl whisk together cumin, chili powder, cinnamon, vinegar, 1 tablespoon of the oil, salt and pepper to taste, and garlic paste. Coat chicken with spice paste; grill on an oiled grill set about 6 inches over glowing coals or in an oiled grill pan set over moderately high heat. Cook until done, turning once, about 12-15 minutes each side.

Sauté onion in remaining oil over moderate heat, stirring occasionally, until lightly golden. Add remaining garlic and tomatoes; cook over medium-low heat, stirring occasionally, for 5 minutes.

Add zucchini, broth, jalapeño, bell pepper, corn, orégano, salt, and pepper. Simmer mixture, stirring occasionally until zucchini and bell pepper are tender (about 20 minutes).

Preheat broiler. In a large shallow casserole, combine zucchini mixture and chicken. Sprinkle with Monterey Jack and broil about 6 inches from heat for 1 minute or until cheese is bubbling.

New Orleans Vegetable Stew

2 cans (14 1/2 oz ea) Cajun-style or
   Mexican-style stewed tomatoes
1 pkg (10 oz) frozen black-eyed peas,
   cooked and drained
1 orange-fleshed sweet potato (about 10 oz),
   peeled and cut into 1/2-inch cubes
4 large bay leaves
4 large cloves garlic, minced
1 tsp dried thyme, crumbled
1/4 tsp ground allspice
1 1/2 tsp chili powder
1 pkg (10 oz) frozen sliced okra, thawed
5 oz frozen corn kernels, thawed
salt
pepper
hot red pepper sauce

In a large heavy saucepan over medium-high heat, bring first 8 ingredients to a boil, stirring occasionally. Cover and reduce heat to medium-low; simmer until potato is tender, about 20 minutes. Add okra and corn; simmer until tender (about 10 minutes). Uncover and cook until thickened to desired consistency (about 5 minutes). Season to taste with salt, pepper, and hot red pepper sauce.

Main Courses

Cube:
To cut into uniform-sized pieces that are about
1/2-inch on each side.

Dice:
To cut into uniform-sized pieces 1/8 to
1/4 inch on each side.

Pork Tenderloin Dijon

1 lb pork tenderloin, cut crosswise
  into 10 pieces
2 tsp lemon pepper
2 tbsp butter
2 tbsp lemon juice
1 tbsp Worcestershire sauce
1 tsp Dijon mustard
1 tbsp chives, chopped fine

Pound each tenderloin piece to a 1-inch thickness. Sprinkle surface with lemon pepper. Melt butter in large heavy skillet over medium heat. Add pieces and cook 3-4 minutes on each side. Remove pork to serving platter and keep warm. Stir lemon juice, Worcestershire sauce, and mustard into pan juices in skillet. Cook and stir until heated through. Pour sauce over tenderloin and sprinkle with chopped chives.

Glazed Ham

1 slice (about 1 1/4 lb) ham steak
1 can (16 oz) sliced peaches, drained
1 can (16 oz) sweet potatoes, drained
2 tbsp maple syrup, divided
2 tbsp apricot preserves
1 tsp Dijon mustard

Preheat broiler. Position oven rack about 4 inches from heat source. Place ham in shallow broiling pan. Surround with peaches and sweet potatoes. Drizzle peaches and sweet potatoes with 1 tablespoon maple syrup. Broil 5 minutes or until lightly browned. Meanwhile, combine preserves and mustard in saucepan; heat until preserves are melted. Stir well until blended. Turn ham, peaches, and sweet potatoes over and brush ham with jam mixture. Drizzle peaches and sweet potatoes with remaining 1 tablespoon maple syrup. Continue broiling until heated.

Saucy Peppers and Pork

2 fresh limes
1/3 c low-sodium soy sauce
4 cloves garlic, crushed
1 tsp dried oregano leaves
1/2 tsp dried thyme leaves
dash black pepper
1 bay leaf
1 lb pork tenderloin, cut into 1-inch cubes
1 tbsp olive oil
1 tsp brown sugar
2 medium tomatoes
2 large bell peppers
2 medium onions

Remove peel and squeeze juice from limes. Combine lime juice, peel, soy sauce, garlic, oregano leaves, thyme leaves, black pepper, and bay leaf. Blend well. Place pork cubes in plastic bag and pour marinade mixture over pork, turning once to coat. Seal bag and marinate overnight in refrigerator, turning pork several times.

Remove pork from marinade, reserving marinade. Discard lime peel and bay leaf. Drain pork well. Heat oil in large skillet over high heat. Add brown sugar and stir until sugar is brown and bubbly. Add pork cubes and cook about 5 minutes until pork is browned, stirring frequently. Reduce heat to low.

Meanwhile, seed tomatoes and bell pepper. Cut tomato, bell pepper, and onion into 8 pieces each; add to pork cubes along with marinade. Simmer 10-15 minutes or until pork is tender.

Hawaiian Pork

1 lb pork tenderloin
1/4 tsp salt
2 tbsp butter, divided
1 red bell pepper, seeded and julienned
1 can (8 oz) pineapple chunks with juice
1/2 c dry white wine
1 tbsp ginger root, peeled and chopped fine
1 tbsp jalapeño pepper, chopped fine
1/4 tsp cinnamon

Trim and cut pork crosswise into 8 pieces. Sprinkle each piece with salt; press into 1-inch thick medallion. Heat 1 tablespoon butter in large skillet over medium heat. Add pork pieces and cook until pork is tender, 3-4 minutes per side. Place pork on a serving plate and keep warm.

Add remaining butter and red bell pepper to same skillet. Cook 3 minutes or until tender-crisp. Reduce heat; stir in pineapple and juice, wine, ginger, jalapeño pepper, and cinnamon. Simmer until liquid is reduced to 1/4 cup. Spoon pineapple mixture over cooked pork pieces and serve.

Chinese Pepper Beef

3/4 c chicken broth
2 tbsp Worcestershire sauce
2 tsp cornstarch
2 tbsp soy sauce
1 tsp sesame oil
1 tsp sugar
1/4 tsp black pepper
1/4 tsp baking soda
2 boneless strip steaks (8 oz ea)
2 tbsp vegetable oil, divided
1 large onion, peeled and quartered
1 large green pepper, seeded and cut
    into 1-inch squares

Mix chicken broth, Worchestershire sauce, and cornstarch together in a small bowl; set aside. Mix soy sauce, sesame oil, sugar, black pepper, and baking soda in a large bowl. Cut steaks into 1-inch cubes. Add to soy mixture and set aside.

Heat a skillet or wok over high heat for 30 seconds. Add 1 tablespoon vegetable oil and spread across skillet with a paper towel to coat. Heat oil for 30 seconds; add onion and pepper pieces. Stir-fry 1 minute, then remove to a bowl. Heat remaining vegetable oil in hot skillet for 30 seconds. Add beef cubes and marinade. Stir-fry until meat is no longer pink (about 3-4 minutes). Add onion and pepper pieces; mix well. Stir chicken broth mixture; stir mixture into beef. Stir-fry until liquid thickens, about 1 minute. Transfer to a platter and serve.

Beef and Pineapple Kabobs

1 small onion, chopped fine
1/2 c teriyaki sauce
1 lb boneless beef top sirloin steak, cut
    into 1/4-inch thick strips
16 pieces fresh pineapple
1 can (8 oz) water chestnuts, drained

Combine onion and teriyaki sauce in a small bowl. Add beef strips, stirring to coat. Alternately thread beef strips, pineapple pieces, and water chestnuts onto skewers.

Place kabobs on grill over medium coals. Grill 4 minutes, turning once and basting occasionally, or until meat is cooked through. Serve immediately.

Italian Cubed Steak

2 cloves garlic, minced
1/2 tsp dried basil leaves, crushed
1/2 tsp black pepper
4 lean beef cube steaks
1 1/2 tsp olive oil
2 small zucchini, sliced thin
6 cherry tomatoes, cut in half
1 1/2 tsp Parmesan cheese, grated
salt to taste

Combine garlic, basil, and pepper; divide mixture in half. Press half of seasoning mixture evenly into both sides of each cube steak and set aside.

Heat oil and remaining seasoning mixture in large nonstick skillet over medium heat. Add zucchini and stir-fry for 3 minutes.

Add tomatoes and continue cooking for 1 minute, stirring constantly. Remove zucchini mixture to platter. Sprinkle with Parmesan cheese and keep warm.

Increase heat to medium-high and add 2 steaks to skillet. Cook for 3-4 minutes, turning once. Repeat with other two steaks. Season with salt and serve with zucchini mixture.

Marinated Flank Steak

1/2 c lemon juice
1/4 c vegetable oil
2 tsp beef flavor instant bouillon
2 cloves garlic, chopped fine
1 tsp ground ginger
1 to 1 1/2 lb flank steak

In large plastic bag, combine lemon juice, oil, bouillon, garlic, and ginger. Add steak and refrigerate 4-6 hours, turning steak occasionally in marinade.

Remove steak from marinade; heat marinade thoroughly.

Grill or broil steak 5-7 minutes on each side or to desired tenderness, basting frequently.

Fluffy Light Meat Loaf

1 lb ground beef
1 onion, chopped fine
6 oz tomato paste
1 tbsp parsley, chopped
1/2 c oatmeal
1 egg, lightly beaten
3 tbsp green pepper, chopped fine
1/4 tsp garlic, chopped fine
1/4 tsp celery, chopped fine
1/2 tsp salt
2 tbsp bran
1/4 tsp pepper
2 tbsp wheat germ
chili sauce *or* ketchup

Preheat oven to 350° F. With hands, combine all ingredients except chili sauce; form into loaf and place in 9x5x3-inch loaf pan.

Cover with layer of chili sauce or ketchup. Bake 50 minutes to 1 hour. Do not overbake. Slice and serve hot.

40

Chinese Chicken With Walnuts

6 boneless and skinless chicken breast halves
2 1/2 tbsp soy sauce
1 1/2 tbsp water
2 tsp cornstarch
2 tbsp dry sherry
1 tsp sugar
1 tsp fresh ginger, grated
1/2 tsp crushed red pepper
1/4 tsp salt
3 tsp peanut oil, divided
2 green peppers, cut into 3/4-inch pieces
4 green onions, sliced diagonally into
   1-inch pieces
1/3 c walnut halves

Cut chicken into 1-inch pieces and set aside. Mix soy sauce and water, then blend into cornstarch; stir in sherry, sugar, ginger, red pepper, and salt.

Preheat a wok or large skillet over high heat; add 2 teaspoons of peanut oil. Stir-fry green peppers and onions for 2 minutes and remove. Add walnuts and stir-fry for 1-2 minutes or until golden brown. Remove. Add remaining oil and stir-fry half of chicken for 2 minutes.

Add remaining chicken to wok and stir in soy mixture. Cook and stir until bubbly. Stir in vegetables and walnuts; cover and cook for 1 minute.

Macadamia Chicken

1 clove garlic, pressed
sesame oil
1/4 tsp dill, chopped
4 chicken breasts, boned and sliced
1/4 lb green beans, sliced
1/2 sweet red pepper, chopped
1 large tomato, chopped
1/8 lb macadamia nuts, chopped
4 tbsp honey
1/8 tsp sesame seeds

Sauté garlic in sesame oil until just fragrant. Add dill and chicken; sauté for about 5 minutes. Add green beans and red pepper; sauté for 2 minutes.

Add tomato and macadamia nuts; sauté for 1-2 minutes. Add honey and sesame seeds. Continue cooking until honey is warm.

Broiled Lemon Chicken

4 skinless and boneless chicken breast halves
1/4 c Worcestershire sauce
2 tbsp lemon juice
1 tsp garlic, minced
1/2 tsp pepper
1/2 tsp lemon peel, grated
vegetable oil

Lightly flatten chicken breasts with wooden mallet until all are same thickness. Combine Worcestershire sauce, lemon juice, garlic, pepper, and lemon peel.

Pour marinade over chicken and cover. Marinate in refrigerator for 30 minutes, turning once.

Place chicken on broiler pan and brush with oil. Broil 4-5 inches from heat source for 3-4 minutes. Turn and broil an additional 3-4 minutes or until chicken is tender and no longer pink.

Yogurt Baked Chicken

1/2 c chicken broth
1/2 c dry white wine
3/4 c leeks, sliced
2 tbsp lemon juice
1/2 tsp lemon peel, grated
1/4 tsp allspice
4 boneless and skinless chicken breast halves
1 c plain low-fat yogurt
1 tbsp Dijon mustard
1 tbsp fresh parsley

In large shallow baking dish, combine chicken broth, wine, leeks, lemon juice, lemon peel, and allspice. Place chicken in dish and cover. Chill for several hours or overnight. Place chicken in broiler pan, reserving marinade. Broil 4-6 inches from heat for 8-12 minutes or until lightly browned. Place chicken in shallow baking pan and set aside.

Preheat oven to 350° F. Bring marinade to a boil in a small saucepan; cover. Reduce heat and simmer for 5 minutes. Cool for 10 minutes and whisk in yogurt, mustard, and parsley. Spoon mixture over chicken and bake for 15 minutes.

Orange Glazed Chicken

1/4 c chili sauce
1/4 c orange marmalade
1 1/2 tsp prepared mustard
4 boneless and skinless chicken breast halves
1 tbsp butter

Make glaze by combining chili sauce, marmalade, and mustard in a small bowl. Lightly flatten chicken breasts to a uniform thickness.

Melt butter in large skillet and add chicken. Cook until browned on both sides. Pour glaze over chicken. Simmer, uncovered, basting chicken occasionally with glaze. Continue cooking until chicken is no longer pink, approximately 8 minutes.

Light Shrimp Scampi

4 garlic cloves, chopped fine
2 tbsp olive oil
1 lb medium-sized shrimp, shelled and deveined
1 c fish stock
1/2 c dry white wine
1/4 c parsley, chopped fine
4 tsp fresh lemon zest, grated fine
2 tsp cornstarch
1/4 c lemon juice
angel hair pasta, cooked and hot
fresh ground pepper

In a large skillet, heat garlic in oil over medium-high heat. When garlic sizzles, add shrimp; sauté until just pink, about 1 minute. Stir in fish stock, wine, parsley, and lemon zest.

In a small cup or bowl, dissolve cornstarch in lemon juice; stir cornstarch mixture into skillet. Simmer until sauce begins to thicken slightly, about 1 minute.

Spoon sauce over cooked pasta. Season generously with black pepper.

Old Fashioned Chicken and Rice

1 lb chicken breasts, cut into 1-inch strips
1 onion, quartered
2 green peppers, chopped
1 jalapeño pepper, seeded and chopped
3 cloves garlic, minced
2 tbsp fresh coriander, chopped
2 c chicken stock
1 c Italian plum tomatoes, crushed and drained
1 tsp ground cumin
1 tsp chili powder
3/4 c long-grain brown rice
1 c fresh or frozen green peas
1 tbsp pimentos, sliced
1 tbsp capers

In a nonstick skillet that has been coated with cooking spray, sauté chicken strips until white (about 5 minutes). Set aside and keep warm.

Bring next 10 ingredients to a boil in a large saucepan. Cover and simmer until rice has absorbed liquid, about 30 minutes. Add peas; remove from heat and let steam. Arrange chicken and sauce over rice. Garnish with pimentos and capers.

Jalapeño Grilled Chicken

1 tbsp oil
1/4 c onion, chopped
1 garlic clove, minced
1 c ketchup
2 tbsp vinegar
1 tbsp brown sugar
1 tbsp jalapeño pepper, minced
1/2 tsp salt
1/2 tsp dry mustard
1 whole chicken, quartered

Heat oil in a saucepan over medium heat. Add onion and garlic, stirring occasionally, until onion is tender, about 5 minutes.

Add ketchup, vinegar, brown sugar, jalapeño peppers, salt, and mustard. Cook, stirring occasionally, until mixture is blended.

Place chicken, skin side up, on a prepared grill about 8 inches from heat. Grill for about 40 minutes, turning every 8-10 minutes.

Continue grilling until chicken is fork tender, about 20 minutes more, turning and brushing with sauce every 5 minutes.

Quick Chicken Marinara

4 chicken breasts, skinned
8 oz mozzarella cheese, sliced thin
16 oz marinara sauce

Place chicken breasts in baking pan; cover each breast with a few slices of cheese. Pour sauce over chicken and cheese.

Cover lightly with foil and bake at 350° F for about 30 minutes, basting every 10 or 15 minutes.

Remove foil and continue baking and basting for 10 minutes more.

43

Salmon Steaks With Cucumber Dill Sauce

2 salmon steaks
1/4 c dry white wine
1 bay leaf
2 tbsp fresh dill
1 stalk celery, cut up
Cucumber Dill Sauce (recipe follows)

Place steaks in microwave-safe dish with thick end to outside. Mix wine, bay leaf, dill, and celery; spread over top of steaks. Cover and microwave on high for 4-6 minutes. Serve with Cucumber Dill Sauce.

Cucumber Dill Sauce
1/4 c plain yogurt
1/4 c mayonnaise
1 small cucumber, grated
1 small onion, peeled and grated
1/8 tsp dry mustard
1/4 c fresh dill, chopped
salt and pepper to taste

Process all ingredients in a food processor until blended. Pour into serving bowl and refrigerate 1-2 hours before serving.

Green Pepper Steak

1/4 c soy sauce
1 clove garlic, diced
1 1/2 tsp fresh ginger, grated
1 lb round steak, cut into thin strips
1/4 c salad oil
1 c green onion, sliced thin
1 c red or green bell pepper, chopped
1 stalk celery, sliced thin
1 tbsp cornstarch
1 c water
2 tomatoes, cut into wedges

Combine soy sauce, garlic, and ginger; add beef and toss. Allow to marinate for about 15 minutes. Heat oil in wok. Add beef and toss over high heat until browned. Cover and simmer for 30-40 minutes over low heat.

Increase heat and add onion, pepper, and celery. Toss until vegetables are tender-crisp, about 10 minutes. Mix cornstarch with water; add to pan. Stir and cook until thickened. Add tomatoes and serve.

Luau Pork Teriyaki

1 c sliced pineapple in syrup
1/2 c teriyaki sauce
1/4 c green onion, chopped fine
1/2 tsp ground ginger
1/4 tsp garlic powder
1 1/2 lb lean boneless pork, cut into
    1/4-inch thick slices
1 c rice

Drain pineapple, reserving syrup. Blend syrup, teriyaki sauce, onion, ginger, and garlic powder; pour over pork and pineapple. Cover and marinate for at least 1 hour in refrigerator.

Meanwhile, cook rice according to package directions and prepare grill. Remove pork from marinade and grill about 5 inches from hot coals, about 5 minutes each side or until completely cooked. Pour pineapple and remaining marinade into large skillet; bring to a boil. Remove from heat and serve pork with sauce and pineapple over rice.

Easy Sweet-And-Sour Pork

1/4 c soy sauce
1/4 c sherry
salt
1 1/2 lb lean pork butt or fresh ham, cut into
  1/2x1/2x1-inch rectangles
1/2 c sugar
1/2 c white vinegar
1 1/2 tbsp cornstarch
1/4 c water
1/4 c pineapple juice
3 tbsp tomato soup
one or more of the following: 1/4 c pineapple
  chunks; few slices raw carrot, shredded;
  1/2 green pepper, shredded; 1 tomato,
  cut into wedges; 1/2 c mixed sweet pickles
2 tbsp oil

Combine soy sauce, sherry, and salt. Add pork; set aside and allow to marinate for at least 30 minutes.

Meanwhile, boil sugar and vinegar in a 1-quart pot until sugar is dissolved. Dissolve cornstarch in 1/4 cup water. Add to vinegar-sugar solution; stir. Reduce heat to medium-low. Add pineapple juice and tomato soup. Boil solution for 15-20 minutes or until it turns from milky red to a clear reddish-yellow. Add vegetables and cook 2 minutes more.

In a wok, heat oil to smoking point. Using a slotted spoon, transfer pork pieces from marinade to wok. Brown meat on all sides. Reduce heat to medium-high and continue to cook for 15 minutes, turning pieces occasionally. Place meat in serving dish and pour sauce over it.

Island Barbecue Pork Chops

1/2 c barbecue sauce
1/4 c pineapple juice
1 clove garlic, minced
2 tsp vanilla
1 tsp ground allspice
6 pork loin chops (about 1/4-inch thick each)

Mix barbecue sauce, juice, garlic, vanilla, and allspice. Preheat electric broiler . Place chops on greased rack of broiler pan. Broil 3-4 inches from heat for 10-12 minutes on each side or until done, brushing frequently with barbecue sauce.

Pork Scallops With Lemon and Herbs

1 lb thin pork scallops
1/4 c all-purpose flour
salt
black pepper
2 tbsp olive oil
1/2 c white wine
2 tbsp fresh lemon juice
1 tsp lemon rind, grated
2 tbsp fresh parsley, chopped
1/2 tsp dried basil
1/4 tsp dried thyme
1/4 tsp dried oregano

Dredge pork scallops in flour seasoned with salt and pepper. Shake off excess. In a large heavy frying pan, heat oil over medium-high heat and cook pork scallops in batches until browned on both sides. Remove to a plate and keep warm.

Add wine to frying pan and cook over high heat, scraping up brown bits from bottom, until wine is reduced by about half. Add lemon juice, lemon rind, parsley, basil, thyme, and oregano. Return pork scallops to frying pan and cook, turning occasionally, until well coated in sauce and heated through.

45

Pork With Cabbage

3 tbsp oil
1/2 c pork, shredded
1/2 medium cabbage, shredded
salt
1 tbsp soy sauce
1/2 c water

Place oil in wok and heat to smoking point. Brown pork in oil. Add cabbage, salt, and soy sauce; stir well. Add water; cover and cook 8-10 minutes, stirring occasionally.

Chicken Breasts With Tarragon Vinaigrette

1 whole skinless and boneless chicken breast (about 3/4 lb), halved
1 tbsp plus 2 tsp vegetable oil
1/3 c chicken broth
1/2 tsp Dijon-style mustard
1 tbsp fresh lemon juice
1 tbsp fresh tarragon, minced
1 tbsp scallion, minced
salt to taste

In a microwave-safe glass pie plate, coat chicken with 2 teaspoons oil. Arrange chicken with thickest parts toward edge of plate; cover with broth. Cover chicken surface with an oiled round of waxed paper and microwave at high power for 4 minutes. Turn chicken and cook for 3 minutes more at high power, then at medium power for 3 minutes until just springy to touch. Let stand for 5 minutes.

In a small bowl, whisk together mustard, lemon juice, tarragon, scallion, and salt to taste.

Whisk in 3 tablespoons of cooking liquid and remaining oil. Transfer chicken to a shallow dish; top with vinaigrette and allow to cool. Serve at room temperature.

Pork Chops With Red Cabbage

3 tsp olive oil, divided
1 small head red cabbage, sliced thin
1 onion, sliced thin
2 cloves garlic, sliced thin
2 tsp dried marjoram, crumbled, divided
3 tbsp balsamic vinegar, divided
salt and pepper
4 pork loin chops (about 5 oz and 1/2-inch thick ea), well trimmed
1/4 c plus 2 tablespoons canned unsalted chicken broth

Heat 2 teaspoons oil in large heavy skillet over medium heat. Add cabbage, onion, garlic, and 1 teaspoon marjoram; cook, stirring occasionally, until cabbage and onion are tender (about 50 minutes). Stir in 2 tablespoons balsamic vinegar. Season to taste with salt and pepper.

Heat remaining teaspoon oil in another large heavy skillet over medium-high heat.

Season pork chops with salt and pepper. Rub with 1 teaspoon marjoram. Add pork chops to skillet and fry until cooked through, turning once. Transfer cabbage to platter.

Place pork chops over cabbage. Remove skillet from heat. Add chicken broth and remaining tablespoon balsamic vinegar to skillet. Stir with wooden spoon, scraping up any browned bits from bottom of skillet. Pour sauce over pork and serve.

46

Side Dishes

Mince:
To cut a food into very tiny, irregular-shaped pieces.

Purée:
To convert food into a liquid or heavy paste with a blender or food processor.

47

Light Mashed Potatoes

5 large potatoes, cut into 1-inch pieces
2 cans (14 oz ea) chicken broth
dash pepper

In medium saucepan over high heat, bring potatoes and broth to a boil. Reduce heat to medium; cover and cook 10 minutes or until potatoes are tender. Drain potatoes and reserve broth. Mash potatoes with 1 1/4 cups broth and pepper. Add additional broth until potatoes are desired consistency.

Sweet and Sour Vegetables

3 c broccoli florets
2 medium carrots, cut into match-sized strips
1 large red bell pepper, cut into
    match-sized strips
1/4 c water
2 tsp cornstarch
1 tsp sugar
1/3 c pineapple juice
1 tbsp soy sauce
1 tbsp rice vinegar
1/2 tsp sesame oil

Combine broccoli, carrots, and bell pepper in large skillet. Add water and bring to a boil. Cover and reduce heat, steaming vegetables for 4 minutes or until tender-crisp. Transfer vegetables to colander and drain.

Meanwhile, combine cornstarch and sugar in small bowl. Add pineapple juice, soy sauce, and vinegar; stir until smooth and add to skillet. Cook and stir 2 minutes or until sauce boils and thickens. Return vegetables to skillet; toss with sauce. Stir in sesame oil and serve.

Summer Squash Casserole

1 tbsp olive oil, divided
1/2 lb zucchini, sliced thin
1/2 lb yellow squash, sliced thin
1 tsp salt, divided
black pepper to taste
3 tbsp Parmesan cheese, grated
3 oz mozzarella cheese

Preheat oven to 350° F. Lightly coat a 13x9-inch baking dish with small amount of olive oil. Arrange 1/3 of zucchini and yellow squash in pan. Sprinkle with 1/2 teaspoon salt, pepper, Parmesan cheese, and remaining olive oil. Repeat layer. Top with remaining zucchini and squash. Bake for 25 minutes. Place cheese slices on top of zucchini and bake until cheese melts, about 5-8 minutes more. Serve immediately.

Scalloped Potatoes

3 tbsp vegetable oil
1/2 c onion, chopped
1/4 c all-purpose flour
3/4 tsp salt
1/2 tsp pepper
1/4 tsp paprika
2 c skim milk
2 lb potatoes, peeled and sliced thin
2 tbsp fresh parsley, chopped

Preheat oven to 350° F. Lightly grease a 2-quart casserole. Heat vegetable oil in a saucepan over medium-high heat. Add onion and cook until tender. Stir in flour, salt, pepper, and paprika. Gradually add milk. Cook and stir until sauce comes to a boil and thickens. Layer 1/3 of potatoes in bottom of casserole dish. Top with 1/3 of sauce. Repeat layers 2 more times; cover. Bake for 1 hour and 15 minutes. Uncover and bake 15 minutes more or until potatoes are tender. Sprinkle with paprika and parsley.

Green Bean Casserole

2 tsp vegetable oil
1 medium onion, chopped
1/2 medium green bell pepper, chopped
1 pkg (10 oz) frozen green beans, thawed
1 can (8 oz) tomatoes, drained
2 tbsp nonfat mayonnaise
1/4 tsp salt
1/8 tsp crushed red pepper
1/4 tsp garlic powder
1/4 c dry bread crumbs

Preheat oven to 375° F. Lightly grease a 1-quart casserole. Heat oil in large skillet over medium heat. Add onion and bell pepper, cooking until tender. Stir in beans, tomatoes, mayonnaise, salt, red pepper, and garlic powder. Heat through, stirring occasionally. Spoon into casserole dish and sprinkle with bread crumbs. Bake for 30 minutes.

Apple and Carrot Bake

6 large carrots, peeled and sliced
4 large apples, peeled and sliced
5 tbsp all-purpose flour
1 tbsp firmly packed brown sugar
1/2 tsp ground nutmeg
1 tbsp butter, melted
1/2 c orange juice
1/2 tsp salt

Preheat oven to 350° F. Cook carrots in boiling water for 5 minutes or until tender; drain. Layer carrots and apples in large casserole. Mix flour, brown sugar, and nutmeg in small bowl.

Sprinkle mixture over carrots and apples. Stir together butter, orange juice, and salt. Pour over casserole and bake for 30 minutes or until apples are tender.

Cheesy Spinach Rice

1 c long-grain white rice
1 c chicken broth
1 c water
1 medium onion, chopped
1 c fresh mushrooms, sliced
2 cloves garlic, minced
1 tbsp lemon juice
1/2 tsp dried oregano leaves, crushed
6 c fresh spinach leaves, shredded
4 oz feta cheese, crumbled
ground pepper to taste

Combine rice, broth, and water in a medium saucepan.

Bring to a boil, stirring occasionally. Reduce heat to low; cover and simmer 15 minutes or until rice is tender and liquid is absorbed.

Lightly spray a large skillet with cooking spray. Sauté onion, mushrooms, and garlic until onion is tender.

Add mushroom mixture, lemon juice, oregano, spinach, cheese, and pepper to rice.

Toss lightly until spinach is wilted.

Corn Chicken Sauté

1 tbsp chili powder
1/2 tsp salt
4 boneless and skinless chicken breast
 halves, cut into bite-sized pieces
2 tbsp vegetable oil, divided
1 c onion, chopped
2 medium green bell peppers, cut into strips
1 medium red bell pepper, cut into strips
1 pkg (10 oz) frozen whole kernel corn, thawed

Combine chili powder and salt in shallow dish. Add chicken and turn to coat. Heat one tablespoon of vegetable oil in large skillet over medium-high heat. Stir-fry chicken in oil until no longer pink. Remove to serving dish.

Heat remaining oil in skillet. Add onion and cook until tender, about 2 minutes. Add bell peppers and stir-fry for an additional 3-4 minutes. Stir in corn and heat throughout. Return chicken to skillet and reheat.

Pasta With Light Basil Pesto

3 c fresh basil leaves, packed and stemmed
1/2 c Parmesan cheese, grated
6 tbsp pine nuts, toasted
6 tbsp olive oil
1/2 c chicken broth, reduced
3 garlic cloves
angel hair pasta, spaghetti, *or* linguine

Put all ingredients except pasta into a food processor fitted with a metal blade. Pulse ingredients several times until chopped coarse. Scrape bowl; process continuously until sauce is smooth. If pesto seems too thick, pulse in a little hot water. Cook pasta according to package directions. Drain and immediately toss with pesto sauce.

Note: To toast pine nuts, spread them on a foil-lined baking sheet. Bake at 450° F for 5-10 minutes or until golden.

Marinated Wild Rice With Mushrooms

3 c water
1 vegetable bouillon cube
1/2 c wild rice
1/2 c long-grain rice
4 oz Porcini mushrooms, sliced
1 c mushrooms, sliced
1 c carrots, julienned
3 tbsp parsley, minced
2 tbsp chives, minced
1/4 c walnuts, chopped
salt and pepper
Vinaigrette (recipe follows)

Combine water and bouillon cube in a heavy pot and bring to a boil. Stir in wild rice and long-grain rice and return to a boil. Reduce heat; cover and simmer for 45 minutes or until all water has been absorbed. Let rice cool to room temperature. Steam mushrooms in a skillet over moderate heat until just wilted. Combine mushrooms and rice in a large mixing bowl; add all remaining ingredients. Cover and marinate for 2 hours before serving.

Vinaigrette

1/3 c peanut oil
1/4 c safflower oil
1/4 c white wine vinegar
juice of 1/2 lemon
2 tsp Dijon mustard
black pepper
1 tsp mixed herbs

Combine all ingredients in a cruet and shake until combined. Shake well before each use.

Avocado-Mozzarella Stuffed Tomatoes

4 large tomatoes
5 cloves garlic, chopped
1 tbsp basil, chopped
2 tbsp balsamic vinegar
4 tbsp extra-virgin olive oil
2 tbsp white wine
1 tsp Dijon mustard
2 avocados, cut into 1/2-inch cubes
6 oz mozzarella cheese, cut into 1/2-inch cubes
chives for garnish
red leaf lettuce for garnish

Cut tomatoes in half and scoop out insides, reserving tomato hulls. Place tomato pulp in a blender; add garlic, basil, balsamic vinegar, oil, white wine, and mustard. Process until blended. Pour mixture into a bowl and add avocado and mozzarella; toss until completely coated. Stuff tomato hulls with mixture; garnish with chives and serve on lettuce-lined plates.

Broiled Roma Tomatoes

8 plum tomatoes, halved lengthwise
1 large clove garlic, pressed
1 tbsp fresh oregano, minced *or* 1 tsp
   dried oregano
4 tsp Romano cheese, grated
pepper to taste

Preheat broiler. Place tomatoes, cut side up, in baking dish. Spread garlic over cut sides of tomatoes. Sprinkle with oregano; top with cheese. Season to taste with pepper. Broil until tender (about 5 minutes). Serve.

Curried Rice, Beans, and Vegetable Pilaf

1/3 c mango chutney
2 1/2 c canned chicken broth *or* water
1 tbsp olive oil
1 red bell pepper, diced
2 tbsp garlic, chopped
1 c long-grain white rice
1 tbsp curry powder
1 can (15 oz) kidney beans, rinsed and drained
1 small sweet potato, peeled and cut
   into 1/2-inch pieces
1 pkg (10 oz) frozen collard greens, thawed,
   squeezed dry, and chopped
1/2 c dried currants
plain nonfat yogurt (optional)

Place chutney in blender. Add broth gradually and purée. Set aside.

Heat oil in large, heavy saucepan over medium heat. Add bell pepper and garlic; sauté 3 minutes.

Add rice and curry powder; stir 1 minute. Add beans, sweet potato, greens, and currants; stir to blend. Add broth mixture and bring to a boil.

Reduce heat to low; cover and simmer until rice and vegetables are tender and liquids are absorbed (about 25 minutes).

Turn off heat and let stand, covered, for 10 minutes.

Serve with yogurt alongside, if desired.

51

Caribbean Rice And Beans

1 can (15 oz) black beans, rinsed and drained
1/2 large red onion, sliced very thin
2 tbsp balsamic vinegar
salt and pepper
1 tbsp olive oil
1 white onion, chopped fine
4 large cloves garlic, chopped
1 c wild rice
3 1/2 c canned chicken broth
1/2 c dry white wine
2 large bay leaves
1/2 tsp turmeric
1/8 tsp cayenne pepper

Combine beans, onion, and vinegar in medium bowl. Let stand 30 minutes, stirring occasionally. Season with salt and pepper.

Meanwhile, heat oil in heavy saucepan over high heat. Add onion and garlic; sauté until translucent, about 5 minutes.

Add rice and stir 1 minute to coat with onion mixture. Add broth, wine, bay leaves, turmeric, and cayenne pepper; blend well. Bring mixture to boil; stir well.

Reduce heat to medium and simmer until rice is tender and mixture is creamy, stirring occasionally, about 25 minutes.

Season to taste with salt, pepper, and cayenne. Spoon rice onto platter. Arrange beans and onion garnish alongside.

Thyme-Roasted Sweet Onions With Tomatoes and Garlic

2 large Vidalia or Maui onions, sliced
    into thin rings
5 small plum tomatoes, seeded, cored,
    and sliced
4 large cloves garlic, minced
1 tbsp fresh thyme, minced
2 tbsp olive oil
1 tbsp balsamic vinegar
salt and pepper

Preheat oven to 450° F. Combine first 4 ingredients in 9x13-inch shallow roasting pan. Drizzle with olive oil and balsamic vinegar. Season with salt and pepper. Toss well. Roast, stirring occasionally, until onions are golden brown and very tender (about 40-45 minutes). Serve hot or at room temperature.

Grilled Zucchini

2 tsp olive oil
1 1/2 lb zucchini (about 4 medium), cut
    diagonally into 1/4-inch thick slices

Prepare grill. Heat oil in a metal measure over low heat until warm.

Drizzle oil over zucchini, tossing to coat; season with salt and pepper. Place on a lightly oiled rack set 5-6 inches over glowing coals.

Grill zucchini for 2-4 minutes on each side or until lightly charred and just tender. Serve warm or at room temperature.

Desserts & Beverages

Rotisserie:
A small broiler with a motor-driven spit,
for barbecuing fowl, beef, etc.

Sauté:
To cook in a small amount of butter, margarine,
oil, or shortening.

Chocolate Pudding Milk Shake

3 c cold skim milk
1 small pkg sugar-free instant pudding mix
1 1/2 c vanilla ice milk

Pour milk into blender; add remaining ingredients. Cover and blend at high speed for 15 seconds or until smooth. Serve at once. Thin with additional milk if desired.

Strawberry Freeze

1 1/2 c frozen strawberries
1 can (5 oz) light evaporated milk
2/3 c lemon lime or orange soda
1 tsp artificial sweetener

Blend all ingredients in blender until smooth. Serve immediately.

Sherbet Tea Punch

4 c brewed tea
2 c orange juice, chilled
1 c concentrated lemon juice
1 c sugar
1 ltr ginger ale, chilled
1 qt orange sherbet

Combine tea, orange juice, lemon juice, and sugar in pitcher. Stir until sugar dissolves. Just before serving, pour tea mixture into large punch bowl and add ginger ale; add sherbet by scoops.

Banana-Raspberry Shake

2 ripe bananas
1 1/2 c raspberry juice, chilled
1 c frozen vanilla yogurt, softened
1 c fresh raspberries

Place all ingredients in blender and process until smooth. Serve immediately.

Iced Coffee

2 c French Roast coffee, brewed strong
    and chilled
2 tsp sugar
1/2 tsp cocoa powder
2 tbsp skim milk
dash ground cinnamon

Combine all ingredients thoroughly in blender. Pour over ice and serve immediately.

Cinnamon Applesauce Bread

1 1/2 c flour
1 tbsp baking powder
1 1/2 tsp ground cinnamon
1/4 tsp salt
1 egg
1 c chunky applesauce
3/4 c brown sugar
2/3 c skim milk
2 tbsp oil
1 1/2 c bran flakes
1/4 c walnuts, chopped

Preheat oven to 350° F. Mix flour, baking powder, cinnamon, and salt in a large bowl.

Beat egg in small bowl; stir in applesauce, sugar, milk and oil. Add to flour mixture; stir until just moistened. (Batter will be lumpy.) Stir in bran flakes and walnuts.

Pour into 9x5-inch loaf pan which has been sprayed with cooking spray. Bake 50-55 minutes or until toothpick inserted in center comes out clean. Cool 10 minutes; remove from pan. Cool completely on wire rack.

Lemon Pudding Poke

1 pkg (2-layer size) white cake mix
2 egg whites
1 1/3 c water
4 c cold low-fat milk
1 pkg (8-serving size) lemon-flavor
   instant pudding

Prepare cake mix as directed on package for 13x9-inch baking pan using 2 egg whites and 1 1/3 cups water. Bake according to package directions. Remove from oven and immediately poke holes down through cake to pan with round handle of a wooden spoon. Holes should be at 1-inch intervals.

Pour cold milk into large bowl. Add pudding mix. Beat with wire whisk for 2 minutes. Quickly pour about half of thin pudding mixture evenly over warm cake and into holes. Let remaining pudding mixture stand to thicken slightly. Spoon pudding over top of cake, swirling to frost. Refrigerate for at least 1 hour or until ready to serve. Store any leftover cake in refrigerator.

Chocolate Bread Pudding

1 pkg (8-serving size) chocolate-flavor
   pudding (not instant pudding)
5 c lowfat milk
5 c French bread, cubed
1 c semi-sweet chocolate chips

Preheat oven to 350° F.

Stir pudding mix and milk with wire whisk in large bowl for 1 minute or until well blended. Stir in bread. Pour pudding mixture into 13x9-inch baking dish. Sprinkle evenly with chocolate chips.

Bake for 45 minutes or until pudding just comes to boil in center. Remove from oven and let stand 10 minutes. Serve warm. Store leftover pudding in refrigerator.

Light Apple Cake

4 apples, peeled and sliced
1 tbsp sugar
1 tbsp frozen apple juice concentrate
2 tsp ground cinnamon
1 1/2 c unbleached flour
1 1/2 c whole-wheat flour
3/4 c sugar
1 tbsp baking powder
1/2 tsp salt
1/4 c canola oil
1/4 c applesauce
1 c apple juice
4 tsp vanilla
1 egg
5 egg whites
1/2 c orange juice

Spray ring mold or fluted tube pan with cooking spray. Place apples in large bowl. In separate bowl, combine sugar, apple juice concentrate, and cinnamon. Pour over sliced apples and stir until apples are evenly covered. Set aside.

In separate bowl, mix together flours, sugar, baking powder, and salt. Stir in oil, applesauce, apple juice, vanilla, egg, egg whites, and orange juice. Pour half of batter into prepared mold. Layer half of apple mixture over batter; repeat with remaining batter and apples. Bake at 350° F for 1 1/2 hours; remove from oven. Allow to cool before removing from pan.

55

Light Lemon Cheesecake

1 c graham cracker crumbs
1 tbsp unsalted butter, melted
1 1/2 tsp corn syrup
1 tbsp water
1 c plain, low-fat yogurt
1 c granulated sugar
rind of 1 lemon, grated
2 c low-fat cottage cheese
2 eggs
4 egg whites
2 tsp lemon juice
2 tsp vanilla
3/4 lb light cream cheese
1/4 c all-purpose flour
fresh strawberries

To make crust, line bottom of 9-inch springform pan with parchment or waxed paper; grease side. Combine crumbs with butter. Stir together corn syrup and water; stir into crumbs until well mixed. Press into bottom of pan. Bake at 375° F for 10 minutes or until firm to the touch.

Meanwhile, drain yogurt for 20 minutes in a cheesecloth-lined sieve. In food processor, combine granulated sugar and lemon rind until sugar is pale yellow. Add cottage cheese, eggs, egg whites, lemon juice, and vanilla; process until mixture is very smooth. Gradually mix in cream cheese until well combined.

Gently press yogurt to squeeze out any remaining liquid. Add yogurt and flour to food processor; process just until smooth. Pour mixture into springform pan; tap on counter to remove air bubbles. Center pan on large piece of foil; press tightly around base of pan. Set pan in larger pan; pour in 1 inch of hot water.

Bake at 300° F for 1-1/2 hours or until edge is set but center still jiggles slightly. Remove from oven; let cheesecake stand in pan of water for 20 minutes. Remove cheesecake from larger pan; remove foil. Let cool to room temperature. Cover and refrigerate for 8 hours or up to 2 days. Before serving, gently run knife around side of pan. Arrange strawberries over top.

Light Chocolate Cake

1 1/4 c flour
1/3 c cocoa
1 tsp baking soda
6 tbsp extra-light margarine
1 c sugar
1 c skim milk
1 tbsp white vinegar
1/2 tsp vanilla extract
Light Cocoa Frosting (recipe follows)

Heat oven to 350° F. Spray two 8-inch round pans with cooking spray. In bowl, stir together flour, cocoa, and baking soda. Melt margarine in saucepan; stir in sugar and remove from heat. Stir in milk, vinegar, and vanilla. Add dry ingredients; whisk until well blended. Pour evenly into pans. Bake 20 minutes or until wooden pick inserted in center comes out clean. Cool. Frost with Light Cocoa Frosting. Refrigerate until ready to serve.

Light Cocoa Frosting
1 envelope dry whipped topping mix
1/2 c cold skim milk
1 tbsp cocoa
1/2 tsp vanilla extract

Stir all ingredients together in a small mixer bowl. Beat on high speed for about 4 minutes or until soft peaks form.

Light Pineapple Upside-Down Cake

1 tbsp butter, softened
1/2 c light brown sugar
3 cans (8 oz ea) unsweetened pineapple slices
9 maraschino cherries
1 c cake flour
3/4 c sugar
1 1/2 tsp baking powder
1/4 c frozen egg substitute, thawed
1/2 tsp vanilla
1/4 tsp coconut extract

Brush bottom and sides of 9-inch square baking pan with butter. Sprinkle brown sugar over bottom of pan. Drain pineapple slices, reserving 1/2 cup juice. Arrange 9 pineapple slices on brown sugar in pan. Place 1 maraschino cherry in center of each pineapple slice. Purée 2 pineapple slices; set remainder aside.

In separate bowl, stir together cake flour, sugar, and baking powder. In another bowl, combine 1/4 cup puréed pineapple, 1/2 cup pineapple juice, egg substitute, vanilla, and coconut extract. Quickly combine liquid ingredients with dry ingredients, stirring just until blended.

Pour batter over pineapple in pan, spreading evenly. Bake at 350° F for 20-25 minutes or until cake tests done in center and is golden brown. Cool about 5 minutes. Loosen cake around edges of pan. Invert cake onto serving platter. Slice into squares and serve warm.

Light Pumpkin Squares

2 c all-purpose flour
1/2 tsp salt
1 tsp baking powder
1 tsp baking soda
1 1/2 tsp ground cinnamon
1/2 tsp nutmeg
1 whole egg
4 egg whites
16 oz pumpkin
1 1/2 c sugar
2/3 c unsweetened applesauce
1/3 c vegetable oil
1 tsp vanilla extract

Preheat oven to 350° F. In a large bowl, sift together flour, salt, baking powder, baking soda, cinnamon, and nutmeg. In separate bowl, beat together egg, egg whites, pumpkin, sugar, applesauce, oil, and vanilla extract. Gradually add flour mixture to pumpkin mixture; beat well.

Pour batter into a 9x13-inch baking dish that has been coated with cooking spray. Bake for 30 minutes or until a toothpick inserted in center comes out clean. Cool completely in pan before serving. Cut into squares.

Light and Fruity Fruit Pie

2 envelopes whipped topping mix
1 pkg (3 oz) fruit-flavor gelatin
2 c ice cubes
1 c fruit, diced
1 graham-cracker pie crust, cooked and cooled
extra fruit for garnish

Prepare topping mix and gelatin according to package directions. Add ice cubes to gelatin, stirring until it begins to thicken (about 2-3 minutes.) Remove unmelted ice. Add topping to gelatin and whip until well blended. Fold into fruit. Spoon into prepared graham cracker crumb pie shell. Garnish with extra fruit. Chill for one hour before serving.

57

Melon Balls In Watermelon Sauce

1/4 small watermelon
1/2 c sugar
2 tbsp light rum
1 c cantaloupe balls
4 c honeydew melon balls

Cut watermelon into cubes; press cubes through a strainer or food mill to make 2 cups juice. Combine watermelon juice, sugar, and rum in a large bowl; stir until sugar dissolves. Add cantaloupe and honeydew balls; toss well. Cover and chill for 2 hours or overnight.

Strawberry-Pineapple Parfait

1 tbsp (1 pkg) unflavored gelatin
1/3 c cold water
1 c vanilla ice milk
1/2 c unsweetened crushed pineapple, drained
3/4 c unsweetened frozen strawberries, thawed

Sprinkle gelatin over cold water. Stir constantly over low heat until gelatin dissolves. Add ice milk and fruits; stir gently until mixed. Portion into 4 individual dishes. Refrigerate until serving time. Do not freeze.

Ultimate Butter Tart

pastry for double crust pie
1 egg, slightly beaten
1/2 c brown sugar
1 tsp vanilla
1/2 c corn syrup
1/4 tsp salt
1/4 c shortening
3/4 c raisins

Roll pastry out thin onto floured surface. Cut into rounds with 4-inch cutter. Fit into medium-sized muffin cups.

Combine all remaining ingredients except raisins; mix well. Put raisins into pastry shells, dividing evenly. Fill each muffin cup 2/3 full with syrup mixture. Bake on bottom shelf at 425° F for 12-15 minutes or just until set. Cool on wire rack; remove from muffin pan.

No-Cook Butterscotch Ice Cream

2 eggs
1 c brown sugar
3 c milk
2 pkg instant butterscotch pudding
2 c half-and-half
1 c pecans, chopped

In a large bowl, beat eggs until light and fluffy. Beat in brown sugar, milk, and pudding mix until smooth. Stir in half-and-half and pecans. Freeze in a hand-turned or electric ice cream freezer according to manufacturer's directions.

Vanilla Mousse

2 egg whites
1/2 c powdered sugar, divided
1 pt heavy cream
1 tsp vanilla

Beat egg whites until stiff. Beat in half of sugar and set aside.

Whip cream, remaining sugar, and vanilla until thick. Fold in egg whites. Pour into metal ice cube trays with bars removed. Cover and freeze. Serve at room temperature.

Banana-Coconut Bake

5 medium bananas
1 tbsp butter
1/3 c orange juice
1 tbsp lemon juice
3 tbsp brown sugar, packed
2/3 c coconut, shredded

Heat oven to 375° F. Cut bananas crosswise into halves. Cut each half lengthwise into quarters and arrange in greased 9-inch pie plate. Dot with butter and drizzle with orange and lemon juices. Sprinkle with brown sugar and coconut. Bake until coconut is golden, about 8-10 minutes.

Bananas Flambé

2 bananas, ripe but not soft
3 tbsp butter
3 tbsp brown sugar
1/3 c rum

Cut in bananas in half, then split lengthwise. Set aside. Melt butter over medium heat. Add brown sugar; stir. Add bananas. Cook until fairly warm and starting to soften (about 1 minute). Flip bananas and allow to cook an additional 30 seconds. Add rum to taste, swirling over bananas in pan. Allow to thicken slightly. Remove from heat and serve.

Blueberry Puffs

1 tbsp lemon juice
2 c fresh blueberries *or* 2 c frozen blueberries,
  partially thawed
1 c unbleached all-purpose flour, sifted
2 tsp baking powder
1/4 tsp salt
2 tbsp shortening
1/2 c granulated sugar
1 large egg
1/2 tsp lemon flavoring
1/4 c milk

Preheat oven to 400° F. Sprinkle lemon juice on berries. Fill 6 custard cups 2/3-full with berry mixture. Sift next 3 ingredients together; set aside. Work shortening with a spoon until creamy. Gradually add sugar, working until light. Beat in egg and flavoring with a spoon. Add flour mixture and milk all at once, stirring to mix. Spread over berries. Bake for 30 minutes or until done.

Low-Fat Buttermilk Bread Pudding With Strawberry Sauce

3 extra-large eggs
1/3 c sugar
1 1/2 c low-fat buttermilk
1 1/2 c nonfat milk
1 tsp vanilla extract
8 slices light buttermilk bread,
  cut into 1-inch pieces
ground nutmeg
Strawberry Sauce (recipe follows)

Preheat oven to 325° F. Whisk eggs and sugar together in a large bowl. Beat in both milks and vanilla. Add bread and let stand 5 minutes. Transfer mixture into 7x11-inch baking dish. Sprinkle lightly with nutmeg. Place baking dish in large pan. Add enough water to pan to come 1 inch up side of baking dish. Bake until pudding is set in center, approximately 1 hour and 15 minutes. Cool completely. Serve with Strawberry Sauce.

Strawberry Sauce

16 oz unsweetened frozen strawberries, thawed
lemon juice
low-calorie sugar substitute
Purée strawberries in blender or processor until smooth. Add lemon juice to taste. Sweeten to taste with sugar substitute. Chill for up to 4 days before serving.

Mango Ice With Tequila and Lime

1/4 c water
3 tbsp tequila
2 tbsp sugar
2 large ripe mangoes. peeled and pitted
2 tbsp fresh lime juice

Combine first 3 ingredients in small heavy saucepan. Stir over medium heat until sugar dissolves and mixture boils. Let cool slightly.

Purée mangoes, syrup, and lime juice in processor until smooth. Transfer mixture to pie plate. Freeze, stirring occasionally, until slushy (about 2 hours). Continue freezing until firm. Let stand 10 minutes at room temperature. Break into chunks. Return mixture to processor and process until smooth. Serve.

Tropical Banana Splits

1 1/2 c strawberries, diced
1 kiwi, peeled and diced
1/2 mango, peeled and diced
1/4 c coconut-flavored rum *or* liqueur
4 bananas, peeled and halved lengthwise
4 scoops (1/4 c ea) apricot sorbet
4 scoops (1/4 c ea) raspberry sorbet
2 tbsp coconut, toasted (optional)

Combine first 4 ingredients in medium bowl. Let stand 5 minutes.

Place 2 banana pieces in each of 4 dishes. Top with 1 scoop of each sorbet. Spoon fruit and rum mixture over sorbet. Sprinkle with coconut, if desired.

Apricot Whip With Berries

6 oz dried apricots
1 c orange juice
2 tbsp honey
1/2 tsp vanilla extract
1 c egg whites (about 8 large), brought
   to room temperature
large pinch of salt
1 c sugar
2 pt fresh strawberries, hulled, sliced,
   and lightly sweetened

Place apricots, orange juice, and honey in a small heavy saucepan; cover and cook over medium heat until apricots are tender, about 20 minutes. Transfer contents of pan to a food processor. Add vanilla and purée, scraping down sides of bowl occasionally. Transfer purée to large bowl and cool. (Can be kept covered and chilled for up to 2 days ahead. Bring back to room temperature before using.)

Position rack in center of oven and preheat to 350° F. Spray 9x9x2-inch pan with cooking spray. Using electric mixer, beat egg whites with salt in large bowl until soft peaks form. Gradually add sugar and continue beating until stiff but not dry. Fold whites into purée in 2 additions. Spoon apricot and egg mixture into prepared pan, smoothing top. Place pan on baking sheet with sides. Pour enough water into baking sheet to come 1/2 inch up side of pan. Set sheet in oven and bake until apricot mixture is firm in center and golden brown (about 40 minutes). If dessert is browning too quickly, cover loosely with foil. Let stand at least 15 minutes and up to 3 hours. Spoon apricot whip into deep bowls. Serve with berries alongside.

Double-Berry Summer Pudding

1 pkg (10 oz) frozen strawberries in
   syrup, thawed
1 1/2 c (about 6 oz) frozen unsweetened
   boysenberries
1 tbsp brandy
1 loaf (10 oz) angel food cake,
   top crust trimmed
1 c frozen vanilla yogurt, thawed and chilled
1 pt strawberries, hulled and sliced

Bring frozen strawberries and boysenberries to
simmer in heavy saucepan over medium-high
heat. Boil, stirring frequently, until slightly
thickened and reduced to 1 1/2 cups (about
10 minutes). Cool for 20 minutes.
Stir in brandy.

Line a 3-cup soufflé dish with plastic wrap.
Cut cake into 1/3-inch thick slices. Cut slices
into 1 1/2-inch wide strips. Line bottom and
sides of dish with cake strips, pressing and
adjusting as needed to fit strips close together.

Trim cake until only 1/2 inch hangs over top
rim. Mix 1/2 cup diced cake trimmings into fruit
mixture. Spoon fruit mixture into prepared dish.

Cover top of fruit filling with cake and press
gently to compress. Wrap pudding tightly with
plastic and compress again. Chill overnight.

Unwrap pudding and turn out onto plate. Peel
off plastic. Cut pudding into 4 pieces. Serve
each piece topped with yogurt and garnished
with strawberry slices.

Banana Meringue With Raspberry Sauce

3 egg whites, brought to room temperature
pinch of salt
2/3 c sugar
4 large, ripe, firm bananas, peeled
Raspberry Sauce (recipe follows)

Preheat oven to 400° F. In a medium bowl,
beat egg whites and salt until soft peaks form.

Gradually add sugar, beating until stiff peaks
form. Arrange bananas on baking sheet. Spoon
meringue into pastry bag fitted with medium
(No. 6) star tip.

Pipe meringue over bananas in decorative
pattern, covering most of banana surface.

Bake bananas until meringue is deep golden
brown (about 15 minutes). Top each serving
with Raspberry Sauce.

Raspberry Sauce

1 pkg (12 oz) frozen unsweetened
   raspberries, thawed
6 tbsp sugar
2 tbsp brandy

Purée raspberries and sugar in blender; strain
into small bowl. Mix in brandy. Set aside or
cover and refrigerate for up to 1 day.

Brown Rice Pudding

3 c nonfat milk
1/2 c short-grain brown rice
1/4 tsp salt
1/2 c milk
3 eggs
1/4 c sugar
2 tsp vanilla extract
1/4 tsp ground cinnamon
1/4 c raisins
1 tbsp unsulfured molasses

Bring nonfat milk, rice, and salt to simmer in heavy saucepan. Reduce heat to low. Cover and simmer, stirring occasionally, until rice is very tender and liquid is almost absorbed.

Whisk 1/2 cup milk, eggs, sugar, vanilla, and cinnamon together in medium bowl. Stir in raisins. Gradually stir egg mixture into rice mixture. Cook and stir over low heat until mixture is just thickened (about 6 minutes). Transfer to bowl and stir in molasses; cool. Refrigerate for up to 2 days before serving.

Orange Sherbet Punch

4 c orange juice, chilled
1 c milk
3 tbsp sugar
2 tsp orange peel, grated
1/2 tsp ground nutmeg
1 c sparkling water, chilled
1 qt orange sherbet

Combine orange juice, milk, sugar, orange peel, and nutmeg in large pitcher.

Stir until sugar dissolves. (Can be kept covered and refrigerated for up to 3 days before using.)

Pour sparkling water into orange juice mixture; stir to blend.

Scoop sherbet into large glass punch bowl.

Pour punch over sherbet and serve immediately.

Café Au Lait

4 c hot strong coffee
4 c milk
6 cinnamon sticks for garnish

Into 6 large mugs pour equal amounts coffee and milk.

Garnish each serving with a cinnamon stick.

Tapioca Brûlée

2 c low-fat milk
3 tbsp sugar
2 tbsp instant tapioca
1 egg
1 c raspberries
4 tsp brown sugar

Combine milk, sugar, and tapioca in a small heavy saucepan; let stand 5 minutes. Whisk in egg. Stir over medium heat until mixture thickens and comes to a boil; cool.

Divide raspberries among four 1/2-cup ramekins. Spoon tapioca over berries; smooth tops. Chill overnight.

Preheat broiler. Sprinkle brown sugar over each pudding. Broil until brown sugar melts and bubbles. Serve immediately.

Strawberry-Banana Shake

2 ripe bananas, peeled
2 c plain nonfat yogurt
1 c frozen unsweetened strawberries

Wrap bananas in plastic wrap. Freeze until firm (about 3 hours) or up to 2 days.

Break bananas into quarters. Combine bananas, yogurt, and strawberries in a blender; blend until smooth. Pour into 2 tall glasses and serve.

Iced Lemon-Ginger Tea

4-inch piece fresh ginger root
6 c water
1/2 c honey
1/2 c sugar
zest of 2 lemons, removed with a
   vegetable peeler
1 c fresh lemon juice
lemon slices for garnish

Peel ginger root and cut crosswise into thin slices. In a medium saucepan, boil water, ginger, honey, sugar, and zest, stirring constantly until sugar is dissolved.

Remove from heat and let steep, covered, for 45 minutes. Uncover and cool completely.

Remove ginger root and zest with a slotted spoon and discard. Transfer tea to a pitcher and stir in lemon juice.

Cover and chill until cold or for up to 2 days. Pour over ice into tall glasses; garnish with lemon slices.

Orange-Scented Hot Chocolate

2 c milk
4 oz bittersweet (not unsweetened) *or*
   semisweet chocolate, chopped
orange zest, cut into three 2x1-inch strips
1/2 tsp instant espresso powder *or*
   instant coffee powder
1/8 tsp ground nutmeg

Combine all ingredients in heavy saucepan. Stir over low heat until chocolate melts. Increase heat and bring just to boil, stirring often.

Remove from heat and whisk until frothy. Return to heat and bring just to boil again.

Remove from heat; whisk until frothy. Repeat heating and whisking once again. Discard orange peel. Pour into mugs and serve.

Light and Fruity Punch

3 oz canned orange juice concentrate
3 oz canned lemonade concentrate
1/2 large can pineapple juice
1 banana
11 oz water
1 qt clear, caffeine-free soda

Blend all ingredients except soda. Pour into half-gallon milk cartons and freeze.

When ready to serve, peel milk cartons from frozen punch and place in punch bowl.

Add soda and serve.

63

Index